CW00766254

REVOLT

CHANGE THE WORLD
BY BUILDING A BRAND.
BUILD A BRAND BY
CHANGING THE WORLD.
--
ALEX LEWIS &
BRIDGET ANGEAR

First Published 2017 by
The TNT Book Company

Copyright (c) Alex Lewis
and Bridget Angear 2017

Design: Paul Belford Ltd.

Printed in Italy by LEGO
Paper from Forest
Stewardship Council
responsible sources

A CIP catalogue record
for this book is
available from the
British Library

ISBN 978-1-9997572-0-5

--- ---

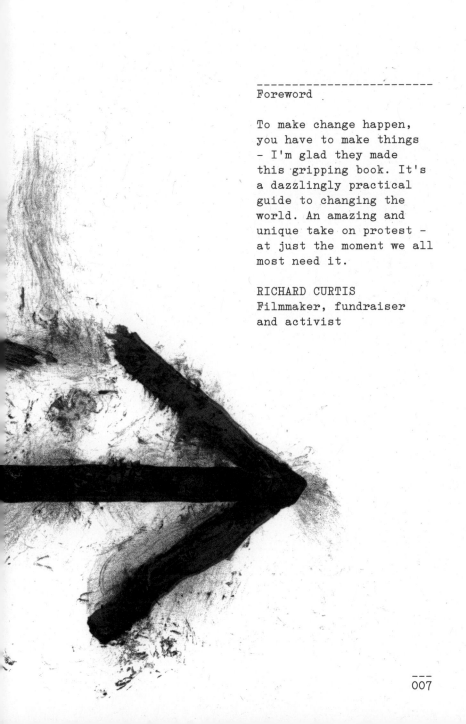

Foreword

To make change happen,
you have to make things
- I'm glad they made
this gripping book. It's
a dazzlingly practical
guide to changing the
world. An amazing and
unique take on protest -
at just the moment we all
most need it.

RICHARD CURTIS
Filmmaker, fundraiser
and activist

The world should be
more revolting

LUCY-ANNE HOLMES wouldn't normally be interested in celebrity gossip. But staring at the third page of Britain's biggest selling newspaper, she couldn't conceal her joy. Of course, it was more about what she didn't see: there was no topless woman.

Page 3 had been part of culture for so long that it remained unquestioned for decades. It wasn't until Lucy wrote a letter to the editor that things started to change. Because when she didn't receive an answer, Lucy got angry.

No More Page 3 began as a simple website where she explained the problems that came from objectifying women in this way. But the petition on it soon received over 200,000 signatures.

Emboldened, Lucy persuaded supermarkets to redesign their shelves so children weren't exposed to sexualised content. She enlisted prominent groups like universities and the Girl Guides to boycott the paper. And even convinced Lego to stop running promotions with The Sun by driving a 40ft topless Lego model to their offices.

Before long, the tidal wave of public pressure forced the paper's owner Rupert Murdoch to step in. Page 3 was a British institution, the pinnacle of media sexism. But against the odds, The Sun withdrew its 44 year old feature. The topless had been toppled.

<u>Melbourne, 2013: Travis is revolting</u>

A moustache-shaped birthday cake is an unusual
request for a ten year old. But not many have raised
$600 million for men's health in that time either.

A decade earlier, and after a few beers in a Fitzroy
bar, TRAVIS GARONE had made a gentlemen's agreement
with an old friend to see who could grow the best
moustache by the end of the month. The month was
November, and Movember was born.

Back home, Travis saw a TV commercial about prostate
cancer. But he didn't know what the prostate was. So
he did a little research and quickly found out how
serious for men's health it can be.

Travis figured he was unlikely to be the only guy
unaware of its dangers. Most blokes didn't want to
sit around discussing their health. But they did
want to discuss Travis's mo. Wherever he went, people
wanted to talk about his upper lip. What if he could
use that conversation starter to raise awareness
of prostate cancer and other men's health issues?

450 people took part in that first moustache contest,
raising $54,000. By the time the birthday cake was
being cut, over 3 million mos had been grown in 51
countries. And Movember had become the largest, non-
governmental fundraiser for testicular and prostate
cancer in the world.

The high school prom has all the trappings of any
other. Until you look down and see that rather than
fancy footwear, every student is wearing a pair
of canvas shoes. And each bears the brand name TOMS
on the heel.

You'd be forgiven for thinking it's some clever
marketing ploy. But this first TOMS FOR PROM has
been dreamt up entirely by a few students at
Ravenwood High who want to share the brand's mission
with their classmates.

Whilst thrilled by the students' initiative,
entrepreneur BLAKE MYCOSKIE is no longer surprised.
It's just the latest in a long line of free
marketing created by consumers who buy into his
mission. Marketing that has helped to create a
billion-dollar shoe company.

That company began just eight years earlier on
holiday in Argentina. Blake was surprised how many
kids lacked shoes. But he was even more shocked by
the impact this had on their lives. It wasn't just
the blisters and diseases; without footwear children
weren't allowed to attend school.

He vowed to do something about it, but could see
that charity wasn't working - donations often dried
up, or provided shoes that were the wrong size.
Blake believed there was another way. He told the
world he was going to start a shoe company that for
every pair sold today would give a pair of new shoes
to a child in need tomorrow. He named the company
Toms for this very reason.

And the world listened to his story. Vogue
journalists listened. Buyers at the world's biggest
fashion stores listened. Bill Gates listened
and labelled him the saviour of capitalism. Most
importantly, consumers listened. And bought over 50
million pairs of the shoes.

So Blake took his one for one mission and applied it
to other categories. Toms eyewear have helped restore
sight to 360,000 people whilst his coffee sales have
provided over 250,000 weeks of safe drinking water.

<u>Mumbai, 2015: Josy is revolting</u>

Advertising executive JOSY PAUL is desperately
seeking inspiration. He's spent days trying to
figure out how his agency's biggest client Ariel can
regain market leadership from competitor Surf. He
knows they need to make the brand famous again, but
also knows this will take more than shouting about
the detergent's cleaning credentials.

Then he spots it. A league table. Not of cricket
teams, or the Premier League. But of gender
inequality. And languishing at number 130 out of
155 lies India. In fact, every Asian country bar
Afghanistan fares better.

And Josy's creative mind starts whirling. What if
rather than taking the fight to Surf, Ariel set
about fighting a more pressing cultural issue? What
if instead of treating people as targets for our
advertising message, we tried to make them the ones
that delivered it?

Fast forward a couple of months and a provocative
film has challenged Indian men to liberate women
from the obligation of doing the laundry. It proudly
states that women should be treated as equal to men.
And in doing so the Share the Load campaign has
sparked a far-reaching national debate about gender
inequality in the home.

It's not just a new idea for the brand. It's a
social movement for the nation. Some 1.57 million
men pledge to share the load. And by shifting
the focus from the stains on clothes to the stains
on society, Ariel earns over $10 million in free
publicity to regain its market leadership position.

This manual will show anyone how to revolt

Make no mistake, a spirit of revolution is in the air. And whilst we've seen governments and oppressive regimes toppled in this way before, we're now seeing how people power can force any type of change.

All over the world, individuals, charities and businesses big and small are applying the same tactics to create their own explosive impact.

Each has seen just how rewarding revolting can be. And you can join them. The tactics they've used are not only clear, they are replicable. By the time you've finished reading, you'll know how to use them too.

Don't think of this as a book, think of it as a call to arms. You'll need a spark to set your revolution off. But from that spark may soon burst your own explosion of change.

<u>When you want to create a change</u>, <u>start a revolution</u>

How did a guy with a moustache become the world's
most powerful voice on men's health?

How did a washing detergent lead a national debate
on the role women play in the world's fastest
growing economy?

How did one woman force an embarrassing U-turn from
the world's most influential media tycoon?

None of these people were tackling worthier issues
than others. None of the founders had more will to
succeed. They didn't have more money. They didn't
have more perseverance.

But they did have one thing. They had people on
their side.

The most powerful weapon on earth is the human soul
on fire. It takes a small spark to get going.
But if you tremble with indignation, you can ignite
that rage in others.

You can rally an army. You can mobilise the masses
to drive action and force change.

Don't pursue a cause, kickstart a crusade. A
revolution will turn that spark into an explosion
of people power.

When you want to start a revolution, create a brand

This might make you uncomfortable. The idea of
linking your noble intent with something as tawdry
and commercial as branding.

But brands are simply devices built to pull people
in. They package up an ideal, an identity and an
image that those on the inside are proud of and those
on the outside can covet.

Powerful brands don't just attract people towards
our supermarket shelves. They turn us into consumers
of football clubs, pop stars and even religions.

Striking symbolism, powerful storytelling and
communications produced by the likes of Botticelli
and Mozart have turned the Catholic Church into
one of the world's great brands. A great brand that
is now the second biggest corporation in the world.

And whether knowingly or not, successful
revolutionaries have long used the techniques of
advertising and marketing. Branding is the
alchemy you'll need to master if you want to make
your revolution a success.

Gandhi told us to be the change you want to see in
the world. But when you brand that change, it
can pull in an army of support that will multiply
your impact. Put simply, the better the brand, the
bigger the revolution.

Revolting isn't about who you are: it's about what you want to achieve

Successful revolutions aren't defined by who starts
them, or even what they're tackling. What unites them
is simply a desire to change something that isn't
right. And this can just as easily be undertaken by a
high-street brand as a bedroom activist. Today's most
potent revolutions are rewarding CEOs as much as NGOs.

Revolting isn't about theory: it's about action

Our aim isn't that you end this book well-read, but
that you will be inspired to go out and create change.
There are exercises at the end of each section to
help create the components you'll need. They're built
for ripping out, photocopying, pinning on walls
and using again and again. You won't find a detailed
academic analysis, but you will find a toolkit
for any practising revolutionary.

Revolting isn't about copying: it's about creating

A powerful gust of creativity pushes forward every
successful brand and every successful revolution.
But great creative acts are rarely born out of thin
air. More often, they are mashups and remixes of
other ideas. You'll need to ape the tactics that have
worked for musicians, religions, tech start-ups,
graffiti artists, sports stars, charities, dictators,
brands, activists, football clubs... and yes, other
revolutions. But this doesn't mean copying. It's
about transforming these experiences into something
new that will make your own revolution distinct.

<u>Revolutions need seven things before they explode</u>

---------------------------   ---------------------------
When we look under the   A FIGHT that defines what
bonnet of a well-tuned   you want to changee
revolution, we see that
they are built around
seven basic components:

---------------------------   ---------------------------
A SYMBOL that lets anyone   A MINDBOMB that catapults
show their allegiance   your cause into culture

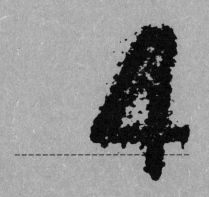   

AN ACTION that harnesses
people power

A RALLYING CRY that acts
as your call to arms

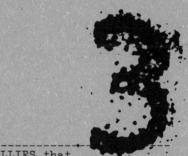

PROPAGANDA that gets
others talking
and writing about it

ALLIES that
you can rely on in battle

Think of this as the Owner's Manual for revolutionaries. You might be able to edge forward with one or
two missing, but to deliver maximum torque you'll
want the seven parts working seamlessly together.

All explosions of change begin with A FIGHT. And the
first chapter will show you how to define just what
you will change. You may already have this first
component in place. But this section will make sure
it's the right one.

The following three chapters are all about starting
your revolution. We'll show how building it around
AN ACTION will deliver the change you're after. We'll
develop A RALLYING CRY as the words that act as your
statement of intent. And create A SYMBOL that acts as
an invitation to participate.

With these foundations in place, you need others to
sit up and want to change things too. And the
final three chapters will show you how to spread
your revolution far and wide.

First, we'll catapult it into the public's
consciousness with A MINDBOMB. Then we'll maintain
this fame through a constant hum of PROPAGANDA.
Finally, we'll show you how to build ALLIES. The
success of any revolution hinges on people power.
We'll show you how to turn goodwill and awareness
into change itself.

A REVOL
IS A BRA
FOUND ITS
T.HE SHAR
T.

THE MORE
ABLE TO C

UTION

ND THAT'S

BAYONETS.

'ER YOUR

BRAND

YOU'LL BE

HANGE.

Always be armed with ideas - you'll find ammunition is everywhere

Each of these components must be fuelled by ideas. You can throw endless amounts of money at your revolution and get nowhere. But throw imagination at it and you'll build a momentum that's hard to stop.

Ideas come from the right stimulus

Undetected plagiarism is the dark art behind any good idea. So feed your brain the stimulus it needs. Combine the experiences of others with your own imagination to spark something new. Fresh stimulus means fresh ideas. The best lead us in a different direction to the one we're used to.

Ideas come from the right conditions

This doesn't have to be complicated. You need a bunch of good people, but the group should be small enough to be fed by two decent pizzas. Each person should bring a different perspective to bear. You need a clear brief for what you hope to achieve. You need wallspace, post-it notes, marker pens and a never-ending supply of coffee.

Ideas come from the right attitude

Getting to great ideas is not even half the battle - you need to make them happen. They begin as a little murmur. But when you get them off the paper and into the real world, they begin to purr. True, the doing might be the hardest part. But it's also when the fun really begins. With careful nurturing that purr can turn into a roar.

When you entertain ideas royally, one of them might be King

Go for broke.

The only way to get to great ideas is to have lots to choose from.

Create alone.

The boldest ideas tend to come from individuals, using the group to bash them into shape.

Explore anywhere.

Do what's expected, then do what's crazy. Find the right answer, then find the wrong one.

Talk through your ideas.

Being forced to explain your ideas will bring them into focus.

Take a breather.

Everyone needs some space for the subconscious to kick in. This is why the overnight test is effective.

But provide constraints.

The best ideas often come from short bursts; set a tight deadline and an ambitious target.

But build together.

Ideas can come from anywhere; withhold judgement and pay attention to what others are saying.

But stay focussed.

Never forget the challenge you're working to as you capture everything.

But create visually.

Sketch, connect and think tangibly. What's on the paper should make sense to anyone.

But commit.

Consensus tends to compromise. The bravest ideas will require someone with the power to decide which to progress.

The_world_is_ready

There has never been a better time to revolt.

A potent cocktail of technology and demographics
provide the opportunity to fix the world's to-do list.

The Internet can spread change faster, further and
cheaper than ever before.

Its tools can be your weapons of mass persuasion.

They can rally your army.

They can inspire action.

The_world_is_waiting

The world is on fire.

An age of anger is upon us, with the spirit of
revolution hanging in the air.

But angry energy with nowhere to go often turns
into despair.

We need fired up revolutionaries willing to pick up
arms themselves.

Make your exit strategy changing the world.

When everyone else is silent, you'll be amazed how
loud one voice can be.

The Fight

When he was contacted for advice by a young, politi-
cally active Indian man, Leo Tolstoy wrote back:

'What does it mean that thirty thousand people,
not athletes, but rather weak and ordinary people,
have enslaved two hundred million of vigorous,
clever, capable, freedom-loving people? Do not
the figures make it clear that the Indians have
enslaved themselves?'

The young man Tolstoy wrote to was Mohandas Gandhi.
And from that moment on, he began devoting himself to
fighting oppression. Your fight should represent
the issue you will rest at nothing to overcome too.

It should be a fight with a clear goal. Because
being part of change means knowing exactly when
you've succeeded.

It should be a fight that's right for you. Because
as well as having the conviction to act, you should
also feel equipped to tackle it head on.

And it should bring a new angle to the issue.
Because an army is more likely to rally behind
something fresh and distinct.

Even if you already know the issue you're tackling,
it's worth taking the time to define it properly.
Einstein once said that if he had an hour to save
the world, he would spend 59 minutes working out what
the problem was and one minute on the solution.
Pick the right fight and your revolution can become
an impossible thing to stop.

10 great fights

Bag it

Make America plastic-
free, one community at
a time

Make Poverty History

End extreme third
world poverty

Campaign for Real Beauty

Create a world where all
women see their beauty
as a source of confidence

The Invisible War

End rape in the
US military

Like a Girl

Keep girls' confidence
high during puberty

Occupy

Make societies fairer

Rainbow laces

Free sport from
homophobia, biphobia
and transphobia

Sports Matter

Save youth sports
in America

Ben's Beginners

Ensure every child
can cook as well as
they can read or write

Hacked off

Create a free and
accountable press

Find what's broken -- then go for broke

The word revolución originally meant to turnaround.
It was only during the French Revolution that this
turnaround came to mean the reversal of society's
problems by the people.

So start by considering which problems need turning
around today. This isn't as easy as it sounds
(it took three years to draw up the UN Sustainable
Development Goals). But we can use the work of
others to give us a helping hand.

We explored institutions like the UN and DFID, NGOs
like Oxfam and Amnesty International and media
platforms like TED and The Economist to see what
others were saying needs to change. Reports from
global think tanks like the Clinton Global Initiative
and the Gates Foundation were added to this list.

Through bringing all of these points of view together, we were able to whittle the world's
to-do list down to nine big challenges relating to
our society, our people and our planet. Each of
these has been divided into the biggest problems
that need to be addressed to create a pool of the
36 most pressing issues.

You'll find them in the compass at the end of this
chapter. Make this your starting point. Each issue
can be broken down further into any number of
smaller problems. And this can often spark something
more novel and distinct.

The best advice is to wander off in lots of different
directions. With your compass to hand it's much
harder to get lost. And you'll soon see that the
world isn't short of things that need turnarounds.

How_to_start_a_novel_crusade:_SPORTS_MATTER

When sports retailer DICKS wanted to tackle the cuts
in kids' sports funding, you might have thought that
health and exercise was the obvious route to go down.

But sport doesn't just benefit our children's
physical health. It creates a sense of community and
belonging. It provides a goal. It takes them away
from other less wholesome distractions. And this is
where they found their fight.

SPORTS MATTER showed the power of sports for kids
who might otherwise be on the streets. By focussing
their revolution on the vital role sport can play in
improving mental health, they carved out a much more
distinctive and compelling movement for their brand.

REVOLU
START
NO ANI

TIONS WITH A

END WITH

A YES.

Start your revolution on purpose

When you're hungry for change, it will push you
towards unreasonable lengths to succeed. And you'll
find this hunger multiplied when it's an issue you
can relate to.

Start by considering what you can bring to the
revolution. Where are your real passions? What are
you an expert in? Where could you exert influence?
If you're a charity, you probably feel that you
already know this calling. But think about whether
it's as focussed as it could be. You might have an
area of expertise, but do you have a fight?

Brands should start by looking for proximities. Think
about where you can really exert change.

Then look to your past. From Guinness to Cadbury to
Toyota, many established brands were born with a real
sense of social purpose. Delve into the archives and
you might find something which is no less deserving
of your attention today.

And if that fails, turn to self-interest. Often a
fight can meet the needs of the business as well as
the needs of the world. Consider whether there is
anything affecting your consumers, your suppliers or
your staff that could impact the bottom line as well.

How to look at your own self-interest: MADE WITH CODE

Google needs thousands of talented programmers to
join them each year to keep up with their staggering
growth. They knew that boys alone were unlikely to
meet that demand. Yet girls were often put off by the
image and stigma attached to computer engineering.

So they launched Made with Code, a revolution to get
high school girls coding. It showed how coding
wasn't nerdy and boring but instead the thing that
underpins just about everything these young women
were interested in.

They have invested over $100 million in the programme,
confident that it will pay back in the future.

How to look at your proximities: 1 PACK = 1 VACCINE

Pampers helps parents give their babies the care
and support they need. And for most parents this
is through the products they sell.

But each year the threat of maternal and
newborn tetanus means that 71 million women have
more to worry about than the absorbency of their
baby's nappies.

Yet the simple truth is that tetanus is easily
preventable with a vaccine. And this gave Pampers
a suitable adjacency. They reasoned that if their
mission was to care for babies, then this should
extend to babies everywhere.

And they launched a revolution to put an end to
these preventable deaths. For every one pack sold,
they'd donate the 4.4p it cost to deliver one
vaccine to Unicef.

In the first 10 years of the partnership, Pampers
funding helped eliminate maternal and newborn
tetanus in 17 countries, protecting 100 million
mothers and their babies.

Lifebuoy carbolic soap was launched in 1895 to combat the germs that were claiming lives all over Victorian England. Over 100 years later, these hygiene issues were no longer a problem in Britain. But that didn't mean they'd gone away everywhere.

So Lifebuoy launched the Help a Child Reach 5 campaign in Madhya Pradesh in India. Their aim was to raise awareness of the importance of good hand-washing habits to reduce child deaths from preventable infections. And everyone who bought the brand helped support this revolution.

Given the brand's history, it made perfect sense. They just reinvented their mission for a different time in a different place. The campaign has so far reached over 250 million people.

<u>You won't find the answer until you ask the right question</u>

You might already have a sense of what your revolution is going to tackle. But to capture people's imaginations, you'll need a fresh take on it.

This means interrogating the issue until it provides clues to a solution. You need to think, think and think again about why you want to see change. Start by bombarding the problem with questions that relate to its who, what, when and why.

Let's_say_you_believe_in_affordable_energy_for_all

Who...

Can't benefit from affordable energy?
Would benefit most from affordable energy?
Doesn't believe in providing affordable energy?
Already believes in affordable energy for all?
Is struggling hardest to pay for their energy?

What...

Does affordable energy actually mean?
Would it cost to make energy affordable?
Is stopping energy being affordable?
Is the impact of not being able to afford energy?

When...

Is affordable energy most important?
Did energy stop being affordable?
Does it need to be affordable by?

Why...

Is affordable energy important?
Can't energy be affordable?

You can see how a relatively amorphous belief
can quickly get under the skin of an issue. The
revolution could just as easily be about energy
for the elderly, price-fixing or affordable
winter energy. And it's suddenly much more fresh
and distinct as a result of the interrogation.

STAND
FOR
SOME

T THING.
R TRIP
OVER
EVERY
THING.

Maximise your ROI (Revolution on Investment)

Your revolution will help you to change the world.
But to have the most impact, you need to consider
where and with whom you can make the most difference.

EFFECTIVE ALTRUISM means getting maximum return
on your good deeds. We need to look for EFFECTIVE
REVOLUTIONING. How can the investments you make to
start and sustain the revolution have the biggest
returns in terms of impact?

Let's suppose we want to help people suffering from
sight loss. In the UK this could mean training a
guide dog for £30,000. Whereas in Ethiopia, there are
1 million people who could be treated for trachoma-
induced blindness by an operation costing £15.
For the cost of training one guide dog, we could
completely cure nearly 70,000 people of sight loss.

This principle can only stretch so far. If you're
a dogfood brand, your revolution is more likely to
relate to guide dogs than it is to the prevention of
tropical diseases. But even within your world, it's
important to ask where your efforts can have the
biggest rewards. Would you have more impact training
guide dogs or rescue dogs?

Establish who you aren't. It's just as powerful as who you are

History suggests that people find it easier to
rally against rather than for something. An enemy
helps bond your followers and multiplies their
determination to sort things out. In contrast to
the common threat, any differences can quickly
evaporate. So think about what stands in the way
of the change you're seeking.

This opponent could take many forms. But if the
adversary feels too familiar it can breed apathy.
Look towards the bigger forces at play. These
can be some of the most malevolent and scary foes,
and often frame the issue in a new light.

Equally you may feel that your enemy is bigger
than any one individual. But if this leaves it
feeling faceless, think about a figurehead who could
represent your ultimate adversary.

And remember that your enemy doesn't have to be a
person or a particular group of people. It could
mean tackling a system like a law or a policy that
protects the problem you're fighting.

You could even go after something intangible.
The most unnerving enemies can be the attitudes
or beliefs that lurk in each of us.

How_to_make_a_figurehead_your_foe: TOUCH_THE_PICKLE

In India, menstruation is often treated as a shameful
curse. Women are discouraged from normal daily
activities during their periods. And this includes
touching the jar of pickle that's found in most
Indian kitchens. It's rumoured that the pickle will
suddenly rot.

This myth offered sanitary protection brand Whisper
their perfect enemy. The Touch the Pickle revolution
successfully called upon women to defy tradition and
taboos by touching the pickle jar.

And over 3 million women pledged to do just that.
Because focussing on this one particular enemy
illustrated the fallacy much more effectively than if
they had tackled those archaic attitudes in a more
general sense.

When she returned to Mumbai after studying in London,
Roshnee Desai realised just how inhibited she felt in
India compared to her time in the UK. Whilst these
feelings reflected how society viewed Indian women in
general, tackling that perception felt daunting.

She needed a focal point. And when she found out
that India was one of the few countries in the world
with separate compartments for women in trains, she
decided to focus on transport.

Roshnee turned the concept of female
compartmentalisation on its head by creating a men-
only taxi. Its aim was to make men experience what
many Indian women face when travelling.

The icon of a coy and covered up woman, usually used
in the women-only compartments on trains, was given
a moustache. The taxi doors were upholstered with
graphics of watching eyes and ogling tongues. The
ceiling was even given a chart of rules which Indian
women are expected to follow, role-reversed for
men: do not wear sleeveless clothes; do not reveal
your undergarments; be home by 7 o'clock...

To drive awareness of her taxi she produced the film
Cover Up, which went on to attract global attention
for her cause.

Change starts at the edges

Another way to find the spark for your revolution is to look at where restlessness is bubbling up.

When you tackle an issue that's on the rise, your revolution can be its outlet, channelling people's concern towards real impact.

This means looking at where society is already straining. But you probably won't find this restlessness in the middle of the road. It warms up around the fringes. So hunt around...

1.   Petitions on change.org show which issues people are starting to rally behind.

2.   Left-leaning media like the Guardian often take pride in being the first to lead the charge through special reports.

3.   Bulletin boards like Reddit provide an early indicator of what the internet is sharing.

4.   Online video being shared today often becomes part of popular culture tomorrow. Subscribe to the YouTube Re:View alerts.

5.   News alerts around the things you think might prove interesting can easily be set up with Google alerts.

6.   Daily bulletins from the likes of This and NextDraft will help tell you what's on the world's mind this week.

7.   Activist_blogs and changemaker sites like
      collectively.org, TED Talks and Good.com
      will highlight the topics other people already
      care about.

8.   New_media_brands like Vice, BuzzFeed and
      Mumsnet are a great source of social tension,
      especially if you want to appeal to a
      distinct audience.

9.   Social_connections can reveal trends bubbling
      up. Use twazzup.com to see what people are
      talking about on Twitter and explore Facebook
      stories to see what people are connecting over.

10.   Caring_people have always been the most likely
      source of restlessness and there have never
      been so many opportunities to hear their
      voices. Medium is home to many of the most
      considered arguments for change.

Always_get_a_second_opinion

It always helps to get a fresh pair of eyes on the
issue you've decided to tackle. Don't filter too
much out. As it all sinks in, you'll be able to
see what the important pieces of the puzzle are.

The expert

Seek out the person or organisation that knows
more about your problem than anyone else. Read
everything they have to say on the matter. Every
interview, every blog post, every article. If
you can, get in touch. Ask them what the one thing
they could change would be.

The enemy

It's unlikely your enemy lies dormant. Look at how
they talk about the problem. What's their excuse?
What don't they want to change?

The forum

The chances are that people are already venting
their anger about the issue online. If they're
not, start a discussion thread and use it as your
own focus group.

The friend

Rant for sixty seconds about what you think needs
to change without coming up for breath. Then
stop and ask a friend to play back what they

heard. You'll soon see the bits they find the most
compelling.

The child

Get a child to do a drawing about your problem. Kids
can bring a wonderful directness to things, whilst
drawing helps to turn the abstract into something
very real.

THE DAN
AN AIM
TOO HIGH
MISSING
AN AIM
LOW AN

SER ISN'T
THAT'S
AND
IT. BUT
AT'S TOO
HITTING
IT.

If you want to really score, aim for a bigger goal

At the heart of every great fight is a clear goal.
It's the single thing that has to happen if you're
to truly succeed.

The best goals act as an inspiring call to arms.
But this means going after something definitive and
objective. You don't want to be left in any doubt as
to when the ball has crossed the line.

Framing this goal differently can often help. When
the Malaria No More revolution set about ridding
Africa of malaria, they worked out that doing so
would save a child's life every minute. Work out
what it would take to see your change realised, then
play around with the maths.

Consider whether a deadline should be part of your
goal. The best are short. They might even seem
impossible at first, but this brings an urgency to
get things done.

And remember that people want to be part of history.
Most of us tend to overestimate what we can get done
day to day, but underestimate what we can achieve
over time.

So go for broke. Set an insane goal. A fight that
has the potential to change the world will multiply
your followers' will to make it happen.

Battles should be small enough to win and big enough to matter

An audacious goal doesn't mean you need to tackle everything at once. Breaking down the goal into smaller, more achievable tasks can often help kickstart momentum.

Let's return to Gandhi. He knew that if he could unite 350 million Indians under a single banner the British would be overwhelmed. But he'd already led the call for self-determination, only to find the fight too daunting for most people.

He needed a different cause. Something that every Indian, regardless of caste or politics, could get behind.

He found his answer in food. And more specifically, salt. Here was a commodity necessary for all human life. And for a country with 4,300 miles of coastline, one that should really be free. But the British were taxing salt production.

Armed with 77 followers, Gandhi announced his plan: he would extract salt from seawater and dare the British to stop him. He marched to the shore through towns and villages all over India. By the time he arrived at the ocean, he'd been joined by 12,000 more allies.

Just as Britain lost America through tea, they lost India through salt. It became symbolic of the unfair taxes and daily humiliations all Indians faced.

Gandhi overpowered an empire, but he started small. A big part of your revolution's success will be picking the right battles. Pit your strengths against your enemy's weaknesses. And when you experience victory, embolden your followers to pick a bigger fight next time.

How to dream big but start small: THE COTTAGE CHEESE BOYCOTT

By 2010, the cost of living was becoming unsustainable for many people in Israel. Insurance salesman Itzik Alrov had even taken to moonlighting as a singer in local synagogues to make ends meet.

He hated the piggish capitalism which was raising prices, but he didn't know what to do about it. He couldn't force a minister to resign, or propose a new economic package.

Itzik might not have known enough about economics. But what he did know about was cottage cheese. And this basic food item had more than doubled in price in a few years.

So he created a Facebook page calling on people not to buy it for a month. Before long, over 100,000 users joined. And within two weeks the supermarkets lowered the price.

But then something interesting happened. People stopped buying shoko, the chocolate milk adored by every Israeli child. Then smoothies. And Swiss cheese. Soon the boycott snowballed into a public debate on the high cost of living.

The government could no longer ignore it. A committee was appointed to examine the crisis and many of its recommendations were signed into law.

Itzik could never have achieved this all at once. But cottage cheese was his Trojan horse.

Find your fight

By exploring what needs
    to change
    (1A)
By digging into your
    beliefs
    (1B)
By identifying your enemy
    (1C)
By making a promise
    (1D)
By identifying what burns
    brightest
    (1E)

Find your fight by exploring what needs to change

What is it?

They say that there are seven basic plots in
storytelling. In a similar way, there are nine big
challenges that inspire all revolutions.

How do I use it?

Think of the nine challenges as a compass rather
than a GPS. They can point you in the right general
direction, but you'll need to do much of the
exploring yourself.

Start with where you think you should be heading.
But keep going deeper. If you can find the issue
within the issue, it may lead to a more distinctive
revolution.

When you've done this, head off-piste. Force
yourself to have a role within a few challenges at
random. Tackling an issue that you might not
have instinctively been drawn towards might provide
a more exciting spark.

WHAT'
NEEDS
TO
CHANGE?

RESOURCES

FOOD SECURITY

EXTRACTION

CONSUMPTION

NATURAL RESOURCES

CLIMATE CHANGE

ALTERNATIVE ENERGY

FOSSIL FUEL EMISSIONS

GLOBAL WARMING

ENERY USE

PLAN

NATURAL DISASTERS

POPULATION GROWTH

INCOME INEQUALITY

TRADE AND DEVELOPMENT

SOCIE

POVERTY

DRUGS AND HEALTH CARE SYSTEMS

HUNGER AND NUTRITION

COMMUNICABLE DISEASES

LIFESTYLE DISEASES

CHILD LABO

HEALTH

E

RONMENT SECURITY

WATER

WASTE AND POLLUTION

TRANSPARENCY

CRIME

TERRORISM AND ARMS

CONFLICT.

FREEDOM OF EXPRESSION

DEMOCRACY

AGE DISCRIMINATION

INCLUSIVENESS

WOMEN'S RIGHTS

EQUALITY

PEOPLE

BIG BUSINESS AND CONSUMER

FINANCIAL SYSTEMS

EMPOWERMENT

JOBS AND LABOUR

THE MEDIA

FEMALE EDUCATION

SYSTEMS

TION THE ECONOMY

Find your fight by digging into your beliefs

What is it?

Your ability to create change is not equally
weighted. It may well be that you could have more
impact focussing your attention on a particular
group, time or place.

How do I use it?

Dig deeper into your cause by exploring the WHO,
WHAT, WHEN and WHY of that belief. These type of
questions can quickly lead to a more distinct fight.

If you're a brand with some sort of existing brand
purpose, start here. For instance, a brand like
Coca-Cola that believes in 'refreshing the world
with moments of happiness' might explore when people
are feeling pessimistic, who is least happy, or
where happiness is most missing from the world.

WHO? WHAT?

WHY? WHEN?

<u>Find_your_fight_by_identifying_your_enemy</u>

What is it?

Finding who or what stands in the way of change can
often be more motivating for the people you hope will
join you.

How do I use it?

Grab a pen and draw the enemy in your target grid.
Or cut out an image and stick it on. Don't worry if
it's not a person - it can be a system, a behaviour
or even a mindset. It simply needs to prompt the
sort of visceral reaction that makes you want to
throw a dart in their direction.

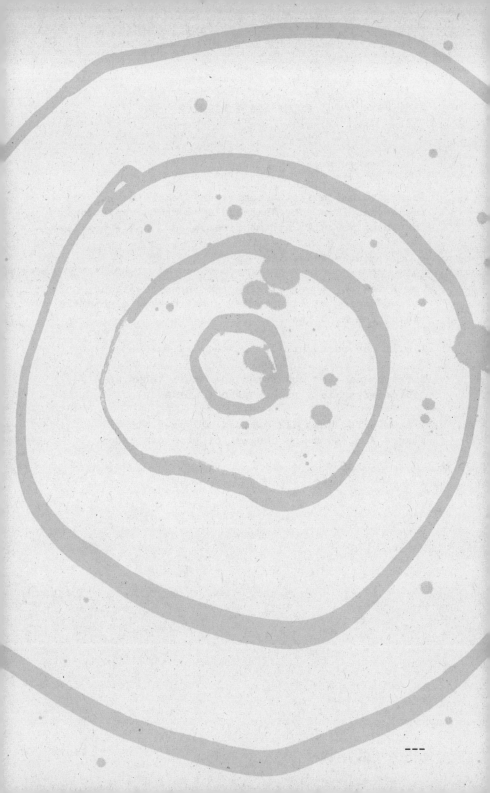

Find_your_fight_by_making_a_promise

What is it?

Your revolution is the commitment you're making to
the world. It's your What Would Jesus Do? wristband.
The thing you will strive towards each and every day.

How do I use it?

Try a few on for size using the three questions
below. Coming at it from different angles might give
you different directions. For example...

I will not rest until... poverty is extinct

I really hate... how women see their looks as a
source of anxiety rather than confidence

I promise... that all men, of all ages, in all
places will know the dangers of prostate cancer

I will not rest until...

I really hate...

I promise...

I will not rest until...

I really hate...

I promise...

Find your fight by identifying what burns brightest

What is it?

Maybe you feel the need to fight on several fronts. If
this is the case, your final task is to filter them.

How do I use it?

First, consider whether there is a bigger fight that
sits above all of these. Just be careful if it starts
to feel too generic or amorphous. For your revolution
to inspire others, it needs to be understood. Your
fight needs to be clear and definitive.

Then draw yourself two circles. The sweet spot will
be where the fight represents a big, meaty issue that
you are equipped to tackle.

Finally, add a third circle and ask how much do I
care? Because this isn't going to be easy; you need a
passion that will keep you fighting when anyone sane
would quit.

AM I
PASSIONATE
ABOUT?
THIS?

CAN I
MAKE A
DIFFER-
ENCE?

HOW
BIG IS
THE?
ISSUE?

<u>Before we move on.... have you found your fight?</u>

The first test -
Is it exciting?

Human nature is to feel before we think. So put all
the rational arguments to one side, come back the
next day and simply ask whether this calling still
gets you worked up in the cold light of day.

The second test -
Will it make a difference?

Project forward to a time when your revolution has
done everything you dreamed it would. How does
it feel? Have you done enough? Are you proud of the
change you've made to the world?

The third test -
Does it make others want to join?

You need to unite an army of followers that feel
the same as you. So grab a postcard and write down
'I'm fighting to change _____ because
_____'. Show it to five people, as different
as you can find in terms of age, background and
beliefs. Does it spark something in them as well?

Notes

The Action

Of all the ingredients a revolution might need, the action you call upon your followers to undertake is the easiest to overlook. And yet your action is what will turn a plea for change into a movement of actual change.

Everyone knows that actions speak louder than words. They turn sentiment into commitment and publicity into proof points.

But they can also help reinforce the sense of community. Humans are social beasts. And we are more likely to do things when we can do them together.

So you need an action that people want to undertake. This might mean mimicking existing rituals. It might mean basing them around a specific moment in time. Or it might mean creating something so exciting and new that people simply have to do it.

Most importantly, you need to mobilise people in an effective way. You might need to raise pressure, or you might need to raise funds. You could be trying to shift behaviours or shift people's minds. Only once you understand how change will be achieved can you start to create the action that will turn people into your lever to get there.

Comic Relief's FIGHT was
to end poverty. Their
AIM was to raise funds.
Their ACTION was to
get people to do some-
thing funny for money.

Movember's FIGHT was
to reduce deaths from
prostate cancer. Their
AIM was to make men
think about it. Their
ACTION was to get men
to grow a mo that sparked
a conversation around
their health.

Nail Transphobia's FIGHT
was to end transphobic
hate crime. Their AIM
was to shift what others
thought about trans
people. Their ACTION
was free manicures
that helped strike up a
conversation.

London 2012's FIGHT was
to inspire a generation.
Their AIM was to
shift the mindset that
the games were just
for London. Their
ACTION was a torch
relay that touched 95%
of the country.

Toms's FIGHT was to
help those without
footwear. Their AIM was
to raise funds for new
shoes. Their ACTION
was to give a pair away
with every pair bought.

American Express's FIGHT
was to support small
businesses. Their AIM
was to shift shopper
behaviour. Their ACTION
was to create a day
encouraging people to
shop small and local.

No More Page 3's FIGHT
was ending topless women
in the Sun. Their AIM
was to raise pressure on
it. Their ACTION was to
create a petition calling
on advertisers to cut off
their revenue.

Lend a Leg's FIGHT was to
put an end to landmines
for good. Their AIM was
raising pressure. Their
ACTION was to get people
to roll up their trouser
legs in a public act of
solidarity.

WWF's FIGHT was to put
the brakes on climate
change. Their AIM was
more energy efficient
behaviours. Their ACTION
was to create Earth Hour
as the world's biggest
switch off.

The NHS's FIGHT was
to end preventable
cervical cancer. Their
AIM was make vaccinating
an accepted behaviour
amongst prepubescent
girls. Their ACTION was
to inspire girls to Arm
Against Cervical Cancer.

<u>Before you act, take aim</u>

People are the power behind any revolution, but you
need to be clear about just how they can create
change. And the first thing to understand is what
you're aiming for.

Top-down approaches mobilise people as a means
to an end. They're for when someone else will be
responsible for the change itself, but your army of
support can RAISE THE PRESSURE or RAISE THE FUNDS
to make it happen.

Both Make Poverty History and Comic Relief used their
following to tackle extreme poverty. But whereas
Comic Relief raised the funds to tackle it on the
ground, Make Poverty History was more concerned with
applying political pressure on the G8 to cancel third
world debt. Consequently, their actions involved
people in very different ways.

Alternatively, change can also be achieved as a
direct result of your followers' behaviour. These
bottom-up actions might SHIFT MINDS by creating
awareness and understanding. It's not legal
structures that stand in the way of racial equality
in football; fans and players must be committed to
kick it out of the game themselves.

Or it might mean SHIFTING BEHAVIOURS, whether
that's buying or boycotting, running or recycling.
Revolutions where the actions start or stop something tend to offer the most direct route to change.

Understanding what your revolution should aim for
isn't always a simple task. For many issues,
there is more than one solution. Not even the most

optimistic of revolutionaries would think that something like climate change can be solved by focussing on one tactic.

Even if you think you could have an impact in several areas, doing so through one simple action will be trickier. Instead, ask yourself what needs to happen most of all and build your action around this.

USE PEOPLE

AWARENESS

1. RAISE PRESSURE

2. RAISE FUNDS

3. SHIFT MINDS

4. SHIFT BEHAVIOURS

ACTIONS

CHANGE PEOPLE

How to tackle smoking bottom-up: TRUTH

Despite the ban on tobacco advertising and restric-
tions on where cigarettes could be sold, a worrying
number of teens were still taking up smoking each
year. The American Legacy Foundation knew that
they were running out of viable top-down solutions.
So they turned to a bottom-up one instead - teen
smokers themselves.

There was little point reminding them that cigarettes
are bad for you. They needed something altogether
more sinister. Something that would really frighten
them. Something as simple as the truth.

Their revolution showed the ways in which Big Tobacco
clouded the facts to get kids smoking. Its genius was
the way this pitted teens against the big, malevolent
tobacco companies who were trying to manipulate
them. They were no longer motivated by a health
message; they just didn't want to look like a fool.

The anger it stoked led to significant declines in
teen smoking. In its first year, there were 300,000
fewer youth smokers.

Cancer Research realised that one top-down solution
that hadn't been explored was the removal of branding
from cigarette packs. But such a change could only
come from government. They needed people to care
as much about standardised packs as they did, so that
public pressure would force through this new law.

Their research showed that plain packs were less
attractive not just to adults but to young children
too. So they simply showed people this evidence
in a compelling way. A film showed kids expressing
preferences based on the packaging in front of them.
To the viewer, they could just as easily have been
choosing sweets as cigarettes.

The film served its purpose. It was chilling.
Emotional. And utterly unequivocal. Over three years
200,000 people signed petitions, emailed their MPs
and visited Parliament to apply pressure. And in
2015 MPs voted in favour of plain, standard cigarette
packs by 367 to 11.

Changing_things_from_every_angle

Often it will be clear that either a top-down or
bottom-up solution makes more sense. But the pathway
to change isn't always so linear.

Take a problem like mental health care. There are
top-down solutions, like the amount of money the
government invests in treatment. But bottom-up actions
that shift the way the illnesses are perceived could
be just as effective.

When this is the case, consider whether you should be
building different revolutions with different actions
to tackle each aim. Because Oxfam's goals are so
broad it has launched Grow, Make Trade Fair, and Even
it Up to tackle a range of different issues.

This highlights the difference between a revolution
and a revolutionary organisation. From Greenpeace to
Nike, many organisations have seen how building a
range of distinct revolutions around focussed actions
can be a more effective way to tackle specific issues.

How to change the behaviour when you can't change the system: BEN'S BEGINNERS

Uncle Ben's knew that teaching cooking in schools is the most effective way for kids to learn. But education systems vary enormously from market to market and as a global brand they needed one consistent action around the world.

So they turned to behaviour in the home. It was clear that parents still valued the idea of teaching their kids to cook; they simply didn't do it. Cooking was relegated below things like craft, music and sport.

And this insight gave them their action. Rather than focussing on the teaching, they needed to focus on the fun, aping many of the tactics used by these rival pursuits.

Ben's Beginners was created to 'teach' kids through a sense of fun, a sense of competition and a sense of reward. They used games, competitions, badges... even a World Record attempt. And cooking became just as exciting as any other activity they took part in.

How to change the system when you can't change the behaviour: THE INVISIBLE WAR

Kirby Dick wanted to help the one in four women who were sexually assaulted during their US military service.

The obvious solution lay in changing the behaviours of those guilty of the crimes. But his research found a more systemic problem, the fact that rape cases were judged from within a chain of command.

In other words, it was as much a cultural issue. And these behaviours were unlikely to change until the structures that protected the crimes changed first.

So rather than putting the spotlight on those committing the crime, the film The Invisible War lobbied for a change in legislation. It was pressure that worked. Rape cases were subsequently taken away from the chain of command.

Dare to act differently

Once you have a clear sense of what needs to happen,
you can create the actions that will make sure it
does. And this is an important distinction.

Raising funds is an aim. Sending a pair of shoes to a
child whenever anyone buys a pair is an action. You
might aim to make men more aware of potential health
issues, but it's the act of growing a moustache that
will get men talking.

Your aim should be actions that are just as distinct
for your own revolution. Something new, something
bold, something cool. Because when you create a unique
action it can become a vital part of your identity.

Not that you have to start from scratch. Comic Relief
didn't invent sponsorship, but they were the first
to ask people to do something funny for money. The Ice
Bucket Challenge used the 'nominate' tagging mechanism
that was first used as part of a drinking game.
Livestrong took friendship bracelets and made them
hip again.

Start with your aim, hunt out inspiration and
create a new action that is going to help your army
of followers leave a dent in the world.

YOUR C[]
IS THE[]
IN SP[]
YOUR RE[]
IS THE[]
INSPIR[]

--- --- .

LLING
TO
RE YOU.
VOLUTION
TO
OTHERS

Raise the pressure with weapons of mass persuasion

When changes in legal, government or corporate policy
are needed, you have to find ways to put pressure on
these institutions. Many famous revolutions have used
iconic placards, marches, petitions and protests to
do just that.

Petitions are one of the oldest tools in advocacy.
But thanks to change.org, it's now dramatically
easier to start and spread them. Every hour someone
forces a change thanks to the 140 million people who
use the site.

It provides a recognised and impartial objective
measure of your support. This can help you get noticed
by journalists on the lookout for campaigners.
Capturing contact details online also means you can
request further action from supporters. And you'll
also have a running tally that helps create momentum
as you hit key milestones along the way.

It's not just petitions. The internet has since
changed the rules in terms of the speed, scale and
accuracy with which you can reach people.

So whilst many of the old tactics still have a role,
the way in which they are now delivered has moved
on. You'll find 49 other tactics at the end of
the chapter. If your revolution needs to raise the
pressure, think about how these traditional protest
tactics could also be given a digital twist.

How to raise pressure through targeting: STOP TAXING PERIODS

Laura Coryton believed the law that classed sanitary products as a non-essential luxury item needed changing. Stop Taxing Periods was built around a change.org petition asking the Chancellor to remove the tax completely.

But Laura also recognised that big business might have just as much influence on government. So she started working with health store Superdrug. The chain agreed to reimburse the tampon tax money to its consumers themselves, significantly adding to the pressure which was building up. Before long, the tampon tax was duly scrapped.

Similarly, when Greenpeace wanted to stop Shell's drilling in the Arctic they chose a different target. Lego sold Shell branded garage kits. So they launched a YouTube video showing the Arctic built from 120kg of Lego bricks. As the camera panned over, the scene was slowly covered in oil.

Lego might not have been the ones actually harming the Arctic. But they were the biggest publicity opportunity. In just three months, over 1 million people had emailed Lego. It convinced them to end the deal with Shell.

Think carefully about who the recipient of your pressure should be. Sometimes others with disproportionate influence can be your lever. By applying a little pressure on them, you may find that force multiplied towards someone else.

<u>How to raise pressure through a stunt: THE POWYS</u>
<u>TAX REBELLION</u>

When independent traders in a small Welsh town
learned how loopholes were used by multinational
companies to avoid paying tax, they decided to
get even.

A town dominated by independent businesses,
Crickhowell submitted its own DIY tax plan to HMRC
which copied the offshore accountancy arrangements
used by these global giants. They effectively moved
the entire town 'offshore'.

As one business owner said: 'We do want to pay our
taxes because we all use local schools and hospitals,
but we want a change of law so everyone pays their
fair share. Until now, these complicated offshore
tricks have only been open to big companies who can
afford the lawyers' fees. But we've put our heads
together, and worked out a way to mimic them.'

The residents made their tax avoidance plan open-
source so that any town could also benefit from their
scheme. And this raised more pressure on the Treasury
to crack down on the tax loopholes, turning a small
local action into a much bigger campaign for change.

How to raise pressure through a gesture: LEND YOUR LEG

During the 1968 Olympics sprinters Tommie Smith and John Carlos shocked the world by bowing their heads and raising black-gloved fists during the national anthem. It showed the world just how much pressure can be created by a simple gesture.

Fast forward to 1997. Despite the worldwide ban on landmines, many of the weapons remain a threat. So on the anniversary of the ban, the Lend Your Leg campaign was launched to keep the pressure up.

The revolution needed to draw attention to the consequences of these remaining mines. But they also knew that the world had become familiar with the typical imagery of landmine victims.

So they too turned to a simple gesture to raise awareness: a rolled up trouser leg. It switched the emphasis from the victim to the supporter. And just about anyone could show their support.

The novelty of the act worked. Not only did it allow people to show solidarity with the survivors of landmines but it created a visible, PR-friendly gesture that put the issue back on the world's radar.

Raise funds with the crowd - make donating easy

Seamless donations

Automatic actions are the quickest way to secure a donation. The very best also brand that action, like One pack = One Vaccine, or Patagonia's Black Friday alternative 100% Day.

Showing beats telling

Making it tangible gives a real sense of the difference that action makes. Adoption schemes that started with animals have extended to 'adopting' trees or even endangered vegetable species.

Crowdfund

If many hands make light work, many wallets make heavy fund-raising possible. Sites like buzzbnk.org and razoo.com are crowdfunding sites dedicated to projects in the social sector.

Redirect your spend

When a donation is a straight swap it removes the sense of missing out. The Tap Project asked diners to donate $1 for tap water. But they'd usually spend far more on bottled. For every $1 charge, diners got a better deal and a child received 40 days of clean drinking water.

Make donating rewarding

Badge it

Something wearable allows the donor to show their
altruism to the world. Whether that's Remembrance Day
poppies, bright yellow wristbands or simply charity-
box stickers.

Bring out the fun

Focussing on the excitement of the action diverts
attention away from the ask. Innocent's Big Knit
sold bottles with specially knitted woolly hats and
donated a percentage of sales to Age UK.

Give something away

The humble charity auction now enjoys a much
bigger potential audience thanks to the internet.
The Elephant Parade raised £150,000 from just 35
celebrity-painted elephants. Sites like
charitybuzz.com and charitystars.com make it easy
to run similar auctions.

Peer pressure

Publicly daring people not to care can quickly force
their hand. Nobody wanted to be the first one
to turn down an Ice Bucket Challenge nomination.
By nominating others with a Facebook tag, it spread
quickly through a tactic people already used.

Shift minds with greater understanding

Many revolutions that seek to change the way
people behave rely on changing their minds first.
And actions are a great way to deliver this
understanding.

Confucius was right: Tell me and I forget, show
me and I might remember, involve me and I'll
understand. From the inside, people can see more
clearly how what they currently think is wrong.

Take The Act of Killing, which sought a reappraisal
of Indonesian attitudes towards the largely ignored
1965 genocide. Simply asking people to talk about
it was met with a wall of resistance. So those
involved were encouraged to act out the killings
in the style of their favourite films: gangsters,
westerns, even musicals. Recreated in this way, the
killers begin to see just how brutal and horrific
their actions had been.

This involvement doesn't even need to be in the
flesh. The Metropolitan Police used a series of
YouTube videos to put you in the heart of an
argument on an East London estate. Each film ended
with two options you faced and the action unfolded
accordingly. This made you see the consequences
of your actions at first hand. An action that was
much more emotional for teens than the constant
lecturing they'd become used to.

If your revolution needs to change attitudes or
beliefs, think about the action that gets people
similarly involved. Because when we do it, we tend
to get it.

<u>How to shift minds through mass participation:</u>
<u>INSPIRE A GENERATION</u>

London 2012 sought to inspire involvement in sport
for years to come. Since most people wouldn't
experience the Olympics at first hand, they knew an
apathy could develop outside of London. How could
these be the Games that touched the entire country?

The answer was to build their action around the
iconic Olympic flame. Simply carrying the torch for
part of its journey was enough to make people feel
the excitement of the Games.

But the real power of the action lay in its military
style planning. The route passed within ten miles
of 95% of the population. This allowed the flame to
be carried by 8,000 torchbearers, showing off the
best of the local area and bringing people together
to mark its arrival.

This also ensured maximum participation from each
local community. Everyone from Brownie packs to
religious groups to bowling clubs were encouraged to
get involved. And the Olympics turned from a two week
event in London to a sporting revolution the whole
country felt part of.

<u>Shift behaviours with education, excitement and</u>
<u>embarrassment</u>

If your revolution requires people to start or stop
something, you need to ask why they aren't already
behaving that way and build your actions accordingly.

> When people don't know, your actions
> need to educate them

The simplest barrier to address is a gap in
knowledge. This has long been the case for public
health campaigns. Perhaps most famously the safe sex
revolution showed the importance of condoms. Durex
recently updated it with the first condom emoji.

One of the most effective ways we learn is through
testing. The Test Your Awareness road safety video
asked viewers to count how many passes a basketball
team made. But most people missed the appearance of
a moonwalking bear. The test showed how much care is
needed when looking out for cyclists.

Even if you're seeking several behaviour changes, it
can make sense to focus on one hero action. Ariel's
Turn to 30 campaign encouraged washing clothes at a
lower temperature. But it reminded us of all the other
small changes we could make to reduce energy use.

> When people don't care, your actions
> need to excite them

A more malign barrier is when people simply don't
care. When this is the case, your action needs
to make the right behaviour fun, cool or rewarding.

Yorkshire Water encouraged fashion-conscious kids to
choose water over fizzy drinks by introducing designer
bottles. Years later H&M successfully switched their

conventional environmental messages to the celebrity-fronted Close the Loop campaign to encourage consumers to recycle their clothes.

But it might also mean a whole new action. Remember that until they grew moustaches in November, most young men didn't talk about the dangers of prostate cancer.

> When people don't feel responsible,
> your actions need to embarrass them

A final barrier is when people simply have no sense that their behaviour is damaging. You need to shame them into changing by making that choice look like the wrong thing to do.

This might mean reframing what the action represents. Rather than focussing on health, the Us vs Them revolution showed the act of quitting as a way of sticking it to the tobacco companies.

Or you could explore the opposite reaction to the one you're seeking. The Fair Trade movement often gets shoppers outraged about unfair trade first. Turn to a spot of judo and use your opponent's strength against them.

How to shift behaviour through educating: MANBOOBS

Argentinian breast cancer charity MACMA needed to demonstrate to women the best way to perform self-examinations, but censorship rules meant women's breasts could not be shown in online videos.

Their answer? Turn to male breasts. Showing their instructional video with manboobs circumvented nudity rules and showed women all they needed to know.

And the boldness of their approach ensured the revolution reached far more people. Armed with a social media investment of just $1000, the video reached 48 million views in just its first week.

Soon mainstream media covered it on every continent, earning PR worth $17 million. It became the most shared and viewed cancer awareness video ever.

How to shift behaviour through exciting: SMALL BUSINESS SATURDAYS

The Small Business Saturday revolution was launched by American Express as a counterpoint to Black Friday and Cyber Monday, which tend to help big retailers and e-commerce but not the small businesses that are the lifeblood of many towns across America.

Rather than guilt-tripping people into supporting the local community, American Express simply made shopping at small stores exciting and rewarding. It focussed on the craft, care and individuality that big retailers could never match.

Their efforts ensured 107 million Americans shopped in small, local, bricks and mortar businesses. So they redoubled their efforts the following year, hoping to establish a new ritual in the calendar.

And in response to this widespread support, the US Senate unanimously passed a motion declaring Small Business Saturday an official day and part of America's national holiday shopping season.

How to shift behaviour through embarrassing:
THE GULABI GANG

The Banda District in Northern India is one
of the poorest in the country, marked by a deeply
patriarchal culture and rigid caste divisions.

Against a backdrop of domestic violence and dowry
demands, Sampat Pal Devi began encouraging women
to persuade their oppressive fathers, husbands and
brothers to change their ways. But she knew that
reason was unlikely to work.

A more arresting action was required. And the most
emotive weapon women had was the very same one
that was being used against them - the bamboo stick.

Being challenged with the sticks forced men to
confront the brutality of their actions rather than
just think about them. They were publicly shamed.
And their behaviour changed much more quickly as
a result.

The Gulabi Gang quickly became a revolution.
Brandishing the sticks wasn't just their action. It
became the iconic symbol of the revolution itself.

Make sure people want to get in on the act

Whether it's raising funds or raising pressure,
shifting minds or shifting behaviours, ask yourself
how the action can ensure maximum uptake.

Can you use mimicking?

Putting a twist on an existing behaviour can bring
both novelty and understanding. Small Business
Saturday was simply a more worthwhile version of
Black Friday. The No Makeup Selfie for Cancer
Research used peer nomination in the same way as Neck
and Nominate. Stoptober and Dry January are just
modern twists on Lent.

Can you use moments?

Focussing actions around a particular moment can
help get people's attention and give actions more
scale. You can incite actions around a month
(Movember), a day (Christmas Jumper Day) or even an
hour (Earth Hour).

Can you use the masses?

Humans are social creatures. We enjoy doing things
together. Part of the success of revolutions like the
Ice Bucket Challenge comes from nobody wanting to
miss out on the fun. Think about how your action can
induce some FOMO in others.

The first act is the deepest

Lend your Leg. Red Nose Day. Earth Hour. There are
many examples where the action at the heart of
the revolution defines it more than anything else.

This won't always be the case. When actions aren't
novel or engaging enough to begin with, the revolution won't have firm enough foundations. But when you
can establish an action that drives real change in
a new and memorable way, there's every chance you can
build your identity around that.

Remember this as you move onto creating your rallying
cry and symbol. These elements will work harder for
you if they unapologetically support and explain the
action. Everything you do needs to communicate just
what it is you want people to do.

<u>How to turn your action into your revolution:</u>
<u>RAINBOW LACES</u>

When Paddy Power and Stonewall learned that not
one of Britain's 5,000 professional footballers
was openly gay, they realised that the odds that
none was actually gay were over a quadragintillion
to one*.

They decided to do something about the stigma
attached to being gay in the sport and turned to
the famous rainbow imagery of the gay movement.
But the clever bit was applying it to something
every player did each time they took to the
field - tying their laces.

Rainbow-coloured bootlaces were sent to every
professional football club in the country. The
idea took hold and players from 54 clubs wore
the laces, from Arsenal to Aberdeen, Everton to
East Fife.

As more players and celebrities joined in, so did
other sports. Soon rugby, tennis, racing and even
boxing were involved.

Thousands of ordinary people wanted to play their
part, to the extent that another 10,000 laces
had to be ordered just to meet demand. All from
one simple adaptation, delivered on a shoestring.

That's 1 followed by 123 zeroes.

Find your action

By building an impact
    plan
    (2A)
By building up pressure
    (2B)

Find your action by building an impact plan

What is it?

Successful change comes from understanding just how
people can have an impact. Before you create
the action itself, you need to know what purpose
it's serving.

How do I use it?

Use the grid to explore what your revolution really
needs to do to create change. One obvious solution
may leap out, but it could equally be that a
combination is required. If this is the case, ask
yourself what needs to happen most of all.

USE PEOPLE

1. RAISE PRESSURE	**2.** RAISE FUNDS
3. SHIFT MINDS	**4.** SHIFT BEHAVIOURS

AWARENESS

ACTIONS

CHANGE PEOPLE

<u>Find_your_action_by_building_up_pressure</u>

What is it?

If your revolution needs to raise pressure, you need
to create imaginative actions that will allow your
supporters to make themselves heard.

How do I use it?

Pick one tactic from each of the five sections and
work out how you can turn it into an action that's
memorable, novel and distinctive. You can't just rely
on a march; you need the kind of march the world has
yet to see.

Then go through again, but this time pick something
you weren't drawn to. It may lead you to a more
surprising place, and that's often where the real
magic lies.

Consumer action

1. Consumer boycott
2. Non-consumption
3. Social levy
4. Preclusive purchasing
5. Selective patronage
6. Alternative markets
7. Alternative economic
   institutions
8. Withdrawal of bank
   deposits
9. Refusal to do business
10.Boycotting connected
   businesses

Obstructive action

1. Sit-ins and sit-downs
2. Nonviolent obstruction and occupation
3. Overloading of facilities
4. Walkouts
5. Boycott
6. Suspension of social and sporting activities
7. Withdrawal from social institutions
8. Stay-at-home
9. Strike
10. Go-slow

Public action

1. Marches and parades
2. Public speeches
3. Letter of opposition or support
4. Mock awards, elections and funerals
5. Delivering symbolic gifts
6. Vigils
7. Protest and appeal film and music
8. Haunting and taunting officials
9. Guerrilla stunts and theatre
10. Signed public statements

Protest action

1. Mass petitions
2. Banners and posters
3. Silence
4. Turning one's back
5. Renouncing honours
6. Social disobedience
7. Destruction of own property
8. Teach-ins
9. Declarations by organisations and institutions
10. Likes, shares and retweets

Political action

1. Domestic embargo
2. Trade embargo
3. Boycott of political processes
4. Delay and cancellation of diplomatic events
5. Withholding diplomatic recognition
6. Withdrawal of membership of international bodies
7. Preclusive purchasing
8. Alternative economic institutions
9. Boycott of elections
10. Boycott of government-supported organisations

<u>Before we move on... have you found your action?</u>

      The first test -
      Is it novel?

The very best actions bring a twist that draws
people in with its novelty. So if it's about wearing
something, what makes this different to other badges?
If it's a new day, what will make it stand apart from
the rest of the calendar? Describe your action to
a few friends and see whether they've seen anything
like it before.

      The second test -
      Is it easy?

All actions rely on uptake. And this will only
happen if the ask isn't too demanding. No matter how
rewarding you might make it, it still needs to be
accessible enough to overcome our natural indolence.
When pushed, would you really do this? What would
be your honest response if this ask arrived in
your inbox?

      The third test -
      Is it effective?

The true test of any action is whether it's helping
to create the change you seek. So return to where
you think the solution lies, whether that's raising
pressure or funds, shifting minds or behaviours. Can
you clearly see how the action you've created will
do one of these?

Notes

The Rallying Cry (3)

Your rallying cry is your statement of intent. Very often it will become the most public face of your revolution. The thing you want people to chant, to write on walls and to create #'s for.

You need the shortest possible way of communicating what you want to change. A phrase that has the power to attract millions of people behind it. The best seem disarmingly simple. But like most elegant things, it's often very difficult to get there. It will mean whittling down everything you could say into the one thing you actually have to say. The objective might be to explain who you are. It might be telling people why you're on this crusade. It might be pointing followers towards your action.

Just don't forget objective number one: to get inside people's heads.

10 great rallying cries

Make Poverty History

Black Lives Matter

Ban the bomb

Je suis Charlie

Yes we can

Dirt is good

Labour isn't working

Make tea, not war

Opt Outside

We are the 99%

The shorter the line, the harder the write

It's easy enough to write vague or formulaic rallying
cries. But your revolution will remain meaningless
or invisible. Often both.

Getting to a really sticky set of words is much
trickier. Especially those three or four words that
haven't been used before. You need something that's
hard to ignore. Something that sounds novel,
or perhaps even a little odd. All whilst remaining
wonderfully simple.

Paradoxically, the best way to achieve this is
writing more to begin with. The rapper Tupac made his
breakthrough album All Eyez on Me through what he
called the fill in the blanks approach. Instead of
perfecting one track, he'd move onto the next and use
the editing process to cut and paste great songs out
of it. Recording sessions were whistle-stop sprints
of up to 150 tracks at a time.

So don't worry about getting it right for now; worry
about getting it written. Rule nothing out. Words
and phrases will keep coming and, somewhere along
the way, they'll start to form into nice lines. The
harder you work, the more you get down, the better
your chances. Somewhere in that mess of writing will
lie your magic.

<u>How to use your manifesto: LIVESTRONG</u>

Writing your argument down in long form can often
lead to the pithy solution.

Buried in the Lance Armstrong Foundation website
was a manifesto on how to live with cancer for other
sufferers. It ended with the phrase 'founded by
one of the strongest motherfuckers on the planet'*.
The title of the page was LIVING STRONG.

This strong, unequivocal, rallying language was a
very different way to talk about living with cancer.
And Nike adopted this aggressive, take no prisoners
stance as the perfect bedrock for their revolution.
With LIVE STRONG the perfect name to boot.

*Remember in 2003 he was famous for peddling bikes
rather than peddling lies.

Start with your wristband

The rallying cry is probably the closest thing to a name that your revolution will have. And whether it's newspaper headlines or celebrity tweets, you want people to use it properly rather than being forced into acronyms.

As the revolution takes hold, those words might also find their way onto T-shirts and wristbands. And unless you have arms like the Michelin Man, you're going to have to work with a certain brevity*.

But this hindrance will come to help. Distilling it down into the fewest number of words possible will bring a clarity and focus.

The most powerful lines typically contain between two and five words. That's it. Not many to write down, and certainly not many to condense a whole movement into either.

Which is why every word should have a role. If it doesn't, leave it off the wristband.

*You'll find the average wristband has room for 44 characters.

FIND
SOMEON
WITH A
JUST M
THEY'
THE SC

GOOD
PEN.
AKE SURE
EQUALLY
OOD WITH
SSORS

<u>Find your line, then stick it to them</u>

The most important requirement of any line is that it passes the stickiness test: it has to be memorable. There's no magic formula, but there are a few linguistic tricks that can help.

Questions and answers

'What would Jesus do?'
Posing rhetorical questions (or their answers) can seed your thinking into the mind of the audience.

Repetition

'United, United, United'
Repeating the key words can really, really, really make the point.

Rhythm

'Keep Calm and Carry On'
Ending on a stressed syllable can make your rallying cry sound more conclusive. In the way that...
'Freedom for Women. Freedom for Men.'...works best that way round, but not really the other.

Juxtapositions

'Dirt is Good'
Collide two opposing statements together to create a tension that surprises your audience.

Alliteration

'Ban the Bomb'
Repeating sounds can turn a statement into a slogan, and a message into a meme.

A little less conversation, a little more action please

The most consistent ingredient in memorable rallying cries is the use of a powerful verb. As we're taught in school, these are doing words. And since all revolutions rely on people doing something, they make a good place to start.

A great verb can help you be more succinct. Hemingway's newspaper training made his writing simple, direct and unadorned. Learn from him. Grab yourself a thesaurus, or head to hemingwayapp.com to spice up your own verb choices.

Verbs tend to have emotion built into them too. Take four different types of walking: March, Skip, Creep, Bound. Each comes with its own distinct mood. March sounds sombre, skip sounds optimistic, creep is sinister whilst bound feels excited and unrestrained.

So when you're thinking about the action, think about the emotion too. Is your revolution angry? Playful? Hopeful? Each will affect the verb you choose.

And remember that revolutions are about the power of what we can do together. Bernie Sanders enjoyed much more success on the back of #NOTMEUS than Hillary Clinton with the more candidate-centric #IMWITHHER. When you say let's do it, it immediately references the group rather than just the individual. Many great rallying cries are about 'we' rather than 'you'.

Leave no room for misunderstanding

In your search for something snappy it can be easy
to lose sight of the most important thing - clarity.
And whilst it can be tempting to adopt clever puns
or flowing wordplay, doing so runs the risk of simply
baffling your audience.

Often the best rallying cries look incredibly obvious
in hindsight. As a rule, write the way you speak.
Keep it simple. When it's chattier it will sound more
human, less corporate and less clichéd. Look at the
lines from the five biggest political parties in the
2010 election...

VOTE FOR CHANGE

FAIR IS WORTH FIGHTING FOR

EMPOWERING THE PEOPLE

CHANGE THAT WORKS FOR YOU

A FUTURE FAIR FOR ALL

It was little surprise that the result was a hung
parliament; each party was saying the same thing -
everything and nothing. Make sure you stay well clear
of anything fuzzy or generic. Focus on unequivocal
declarations.

Perhaps the problem arose because politics tends
to rely on decisions by committee. If you want the
best rallying cry, get one person to write it. And
don't rule by consensus. A better decision-maker
can usually be found by approaching a stranger in a
coffee shop.

<u>How to use layman's terms: MAKE POVERTY HISTORY</u>

Make Poverty History looks like a classic rallying
cry because it contains three simple ingredients: a
verb, a problem and a solution.

Make - A simple verb.

Poverty - The problem it wants to tackle.

History - The ultimate aim of the campaign.

Before Make Poverty History was arrived at, the other
option considered was Make Poverty Extinct. On paper,
it was clever - it had that same sense of certainty
and played off the fact that this generation could
be known for eradicating something bad, rather than
a plant or wildlife species.

But it just didn't sound right. It was a bit clunky
and awkward. A little too clever. And when Extinct
was exchanged for History, suddenly everything seemed
to click.

Make it simple but significant

When people have to commit words to paper, they have
a tendency to start using a different voice from
the one they speak in. Longer words suddenly appear,
in the hope that they sound more impressive. But more
often the opposite tends to be the case.

Really challenge the words you're considering.
Continue this list. Write down the words you're
playing with and keep scratching them out until you
get to the simplest expression.

~~demonstrate~~ show

~~endeavour~~ try

~~require~~ need

~~additional~~ extra

~~superior~~ better

~~sufficient~~ enough

~~request~~ ask

~~inform~~ tell

Always look on the bright side of life

You'll notice that many of the best rallying cries
are framed in the positive. It's not that getting
angry is wrong (we'll come to that shortly) but
optimism and generosity tend to be more rallying
emotions.

James Druckman was a political scientist who found
that people were willing to support a programme
that claimed 95% employment but then oppose the
same programme when its claim was 5% unemployment.
It's not that we're poor at maths. We simply turn
our heads towards the light like sunflowers.

Persil could have focussed on all the things kids
were missing out on by spending less time outside.
But they chose to frame things in the positive. Dirt
is Good spoke to the possibility of the outdoors
rather than guilt-tripping parents already feeling
under pressure.

So draw people in with the sense of hope. Rather than
appeal to the angry minority, inspire the optimistic
majority who respond to their desire to improve.
Before you try to pander to someone's guilt, see if
you can unleash their kindness.

WHA'

STAND

CAN

A IMP

AS W

STAN

YOU
AGAINST JUST
TANT
T YOU
FOR.

<u>Sometimes_you_have_to_get_angry_to_get_things_done</u>

On the other hand, it can be a lot easier when there
is a potent enemy to stand against. If you tremble
with indignation, you can ignite that rage in others.

The best place for a negative statement tends to be
when there is something definitive to aim for. Bombs
shouldn'.t exist under any circumstances rather
than under certain conditions, so Ban the Bomb.
Drugs shouldn't even be considered, so Just Say No.

If your revolution is more about ending something
than it is about starting, you may find a role
for that fury in your rallying cry. But when you do
go down this route, make it unequivocal.

Find your rallying cry

By creating new ways to
    say the same thing
    (3A)
By writing your TED talk
    (3B)
By playing with verbs
    (3C)
By creating a hashtag
    (3D)

Find your rallying cry by creating new ways to say the same thing

What is it?

People want to be a part of revolutions to be involved in a transformation. They want to be part of change.

How do I use it?

The answer can often be found by re-expressing your fight in a different way. Don't worry about snappiness to begin with. Just get everything down by asking what you want to achieve in different ways.

Once you've started filling up the page, look for words, phrases or statements that leap off it. If they sound good, consider whether they carry the same meaning. Are they distinctive? Is it still clear what you're trying to achieve?

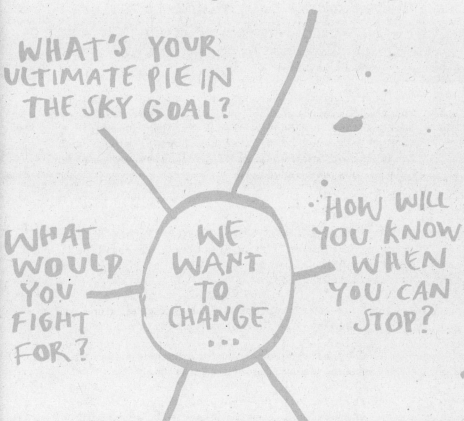

WHAT DO YOU WANT PEOPLE TO DO?

WHAT'S YOUR ULTIMATE PIE IN THE SKY GOAL?

HOW WILL YOU KNOW WHEN YOU CAN STOP?

WE WANT TO CHANGE ...

WHAT WOULD YOU FIGHT FOR?

WHY ON EARTH ARE YOU DOING THIS?

WHAT ONE SPECIFIC THING WOULD YOU LIKE TO SEE CHANGED?

Find_your_rallying_cry_by_writing_your_TED_talk

What is it?

The Negro and the American Dream was an 18-minute speech, containing 1,660 words. But four will never be forgotten - I have a dream. Freeing yourself from the tyranny of writing the perfect slogan and focussing on another form of persuasive writing can help unlock new language.

How do I use it?

Write a five minute TED talk that sells the world on your revolution. Think of it as your political manifesto. There are three tricks that you see time and again in the best:

- They tell stories. So use juxtapositions and take the listener on a journey.

- They have a conversation. So use personal anecdotes to lighten things up.

- They deliver jaw-dropping moments. So teach the audience something new with arresting, surprising and shocking revelations.

Again, once you've finished go back over it to see which words and phrases leap out.

Find_your_rallying_cry_by_playing_with_verbs

What is it?

Since getting people to do something is the ultimate
goal of any revolution, the most consistent
ingredient in the best rallying cries tends to be a
powerful verb.

How do I use it?

1. Generate a list of all the verbs you think
    might be relevant (we've given you 500 of the
    best to get you going). Write one per post-it
    note and stick them up on a wall.

2. Next, think about how to describe the specific
    issue you're trying to solve. Again one per
    post-it (ideally a different coloured set) and
    then stick these up, too.

3. Do the same for the goal or desired outcome
    of your task.

Repeat this until you've filled the walls. It should
now be much easier to make connections between words
and construct new phrases out of them.

They still need to work together with a certain
rhythm and poetry so feel free to bend the rules.
Don't worry if it's not three words, or if it doesn't
have a verb. Above all, it needs to sound right.

```
--------
A            battle      challenge   damage       expect
accelerate   bear        change      dance        explain
accept       beat        charge      dare         explode
achieve      become      chase       deal         express
acquire      beg         cheat       decide       --------
adapt        begin       check       delay        F
add          behave      cheer       deliver      face
address      belong      choose      demonstrate  fail
admit        bend        chop        depend       fasten
adopt        bet         claim       design       fear
agree        bid         clap        destroy      feed
alert        bite        clean       dig          feel
allow        bleed       clear       direct       fetch
announce     bless       cling       disagree     fight
annoy        blow        close       discover     fill
answer       bolt        collect     dive         find
apologise    bomb        colour      divide       fire
appear       borrow      come        do           fit
applaud      bounce      compare     doubt        fix
appreciate   box         compete     drag         flash
approve      brake       complain    drain        flee
argue        break       complete    dream        fling
arrange      breathe     confuse     drive        float
arrest       bring       connect     drop         flow
arrive       bruise      consider    drum         fly
ask          build       continue    dry          fold
assist       bump        control     --------     follow
attack       burn        copy        E            fool
attain       burst       count       earn         force
attempt      bury        cover       eat          forget
attract      bust        crack       empty        forgive
avoid        buy         crash       end          freeze
awake        --------    create      endure       frighten
--------     C           cross       enjoy        fry
B            call        crush       enter        --------
back         care        cry         escape       G
ban          carry       cure        examine      gather
bang         carve       cut         excite       get
bare         catch       --------    excuse       give
bat          cause       D           exist        ...
```

---

glue	increase	lend	number	post
go	influence	let	_____	pour
govern	inject	lie	O	pray
grab	inspire	light	obey	predict
greet	instruct	like	object	prefer
grip	intend	list	offend	prepare
grow	interest	listen	offer	present
guarantee	interrupt	live	open	press
guard	introduce	load	order	pretend
guess	invent	lock	overtake	prevent
guide	invite	long	overthrow	print
_____	itch	look	owe	promise
H	_____	lose	own	propose
hammer	J	love	_____	protect
hand	jail	_____	P	provide
handle	jam	M	pack	pull
hang	join	make	paint	pump
happen	joke	manage	park	punch
harm	judge	map	part	punish
hate	jump	march	pass	push
head	justify	mark	pat	put
heal	_____	match	pause	_____
heap	K	matter	pay	Q
hear	keep	mean	peck	question
heat	kick	meet	pedal	quit
help	kill	mend	peel	_____
hide	kiss	mine	perform	R
hit	knock	mislead	permit	race
hold	know	miss	persuade	raise
hope	_____	mistake	phone	rate
hug	L	mix	pick	reach
hunt	label	move	pinch	read
hurry	land	murder	place	recommend
hurt	last	_____	plan	record
_____	laugh	N	play	recruit
I	launch	nail	plead	reduce
ignore	lead	name	plug	refuse
imagine	leap	need	point	reject
improve	learn	nod	poke	relax
include	leave	notice	pop	release

rely	sell	spot	teach	walk
remain	send	spray	tear	want
remember	set	spread	tell	warn
remind	settle	squash	terrify	waste
remove	shape	squeeze	test	watch
repair	share	stamp	thank	wave
repeat	shine	stand	think	wear
reply	shock	start	thrive	weigh
request	shoot	stay	throw	welcome
rescue	shop	steal	thrust	whip
return	show	step	tick	whisper
review	shrink	stick	tie	win
rid	shut	sting	tip	wipe
rinse	sign	stop	touch	wish
rise	sing	store	trade	work
risk	sink	strap	transform	worry
rob	sit	stretch	trap	wreck
rock	skip	strike	treat	write
roll	slap	strip	trick	_____
rot	slay	study	trip	X-Z
ruin	sleep	stuff	trust	yell
rule	slide	suck	try	zip
run	sling	suffer	tug	zoom
rush	slip	suggest	turn	
_____	slow	supply	_____	
S	smash	support	U	
sack	smell	surprise	understand	
save	smile	surround	unite	
say	snatch	swear	unlock	
scare	soak	sweat	unpack	
scrape	solve	swim	upset	
scratch	sort	swing	use	
scream	sound	switch	_____	
screw	spare	_____	V	
scrub	spark	T	vanish	
seal	speak	take	visit	
search	speed	talk	_____	
see	spend	tap	W	
seek	spill	target	wait	
select	spoil	taste	wake	

<u>Find your rallying cry by creating a hashtag</u>

What is it?

One hour after gunmen walked into the offices of the
satirical magazine Charlie Hebdo, music journalist
Joachim Roncin posted the hashtag #Jesuischarlie.
A day later and the slogan had been adopted worldwide
as a statement of resolve. Hashtags are a powerful
way to badge and share a belief.

How do I use it?

Writing the hashtag serves two purposes - first,
they're built for sharing. You need to get into the
habit of creating something that will be picked up
and made famous. And secondly, they are constrained.
Remember your 44-character wristband limit.

--

--

--

--

--

--

--

--

--

<u>Before we move on.... have you found your</u>
<u>rallying cry?</u>

       The first test -
       Is it memorable?

The overnight test will determine whether or not
you have created something truly memorable.
When you wake up, can you remember what you wrote
the previous day? Does it still excite you as
much as it did the first time you heard it? Does
it still feel completely right?

       The second test -
       Is it taken?

You want to ensure your revolution is distinct and
ownable. Do a quick Google search to ensure your
rallying cry isn't already in use. See whether the
domain name is taken. And check whether anyone
uses similar hashtags.

       The third test -
       Is it simple?

Brevity will be your best friend. Hopefully you've
got something that is two to five words of gold-
dust. But double-check. Can you write it on that
wristband? Will it fit into a hashtag?

Notes

The Symbol

Whether it's on the web or on the streets, in order
for people to gather around a revolution they
need something tangible. Nothing does this better
than iconography, images and symbols. It's why so
many become shorthand for revolution itself.

Any football fan will tell you that symbols separate
the insiders from the outsiders. They act as the
badge of honour that strengthens the community. You
can use them to build your own fan club. And when you
inspire people to use them in this way it turns your
own followers into both the medium and the message.

But perhaps more than anything, a great symbol can
be an invitation to participate. Create one that's
built for sharing and it can be the first thing that
helps the revolution to spread.

10_great_symbols

Good_symbols_copy,_great_symbols_steal

When it comes to creating a symbol, there is one
trick you'll find more useful than any other -
stealing.

Simply copying and pasting what has worked for others
won't get you very far. But with the imagination to
tweak and reinterpret things, you can use the visual
stimulus that's all around us as your inspiration
towards something truly iconic.

Start by looking for shortcuts that carry meaning
elsewhere. Perhaps another symbol, or a metaphor
that captures the change you want to see. These
can then be played with to build off that existing
understanding.

And don't be afraid to go beyond the visual. You'll
find inspiration in songs, poses or even gestures.

How_to_borrow_from_art:_BAN_THE_BOMB

Gerald Holtom based the world's best known protest
symbol around a painting that had inspired him whilst
he was studying the Spanish artist Goya.

The simple line drawing he made was 'representative
of an individual in despair, with palms outstretched
and downwards in the manner of Goya's peasant before
the firing squad'.

He formalised the drawing on a small piece of paper
by putting a circle around it and pinning it to the
lapel of his jacket. It was only that evening when
the post office clerk asked what the badge was that
he realised he was onto something.

The icon was first used for the Campaign for Nuclear
Disarmament during a 1958 march. But to this day
the helplessness of that person's outstretched arms
continue to be used in peace protests the world over.

Leonie
YOU'RE BEAUTIFUL
Hannah ♡ Simon
09-03-09
2010-2010
ALLED
I WILL BE BACK BEFORE THIS WRITING WILL BE CANCELED TO ASK YOU TO BE MY WIFE
best

How to borrow from shared meaning: THE RED NOSE

Like many people, screenwriter Richard Curtis and comedian Lenny Henry felt compelled to do something about the 1984 Ethiopian famine.

Whilst many charities focussed on the suffering, they decided it would be more effective to put the fun into fundraising. And this novel way of raising money provided the meaning for their symbol.

Given that Comic Relief was all about doing funny things for money, they used a clown's red nose to symbolise the fact that anyone could play their part. Held every two years, Red Nose Day has since become something of a British institution.

And over all those years and all those activities, everyone is seen wearing a Red Nose. There have been 29 variations to date, but their shared meaning ensures each one symbolises the revolution in the same way.

<u>How to borrow from metaphors: #SAFETYPIN</u>

Following the UK's decision to leave the EU, there was a 57% rise in reports of hate crime, mostly aimed at immigrants.

Another immigrant, Allison, an American woman living in London, was dismayed by the outpouring of racist abuse following the vote. But she also came up with a clever symbol of support.

Her idea was to wear an empty safety pin. Not just to symbolise solidarity against racism, but to show that she was willing to be part of the solution. The pin said she'd confront racist behaviour and be there for anyone who was a victim. It was a metaphor for the safety she was willing to offer.

Inexpensive and free from language or political slogans, the safety pin let anyone who felt threatened know that they weren't alone and their right to be in the UK was supported.

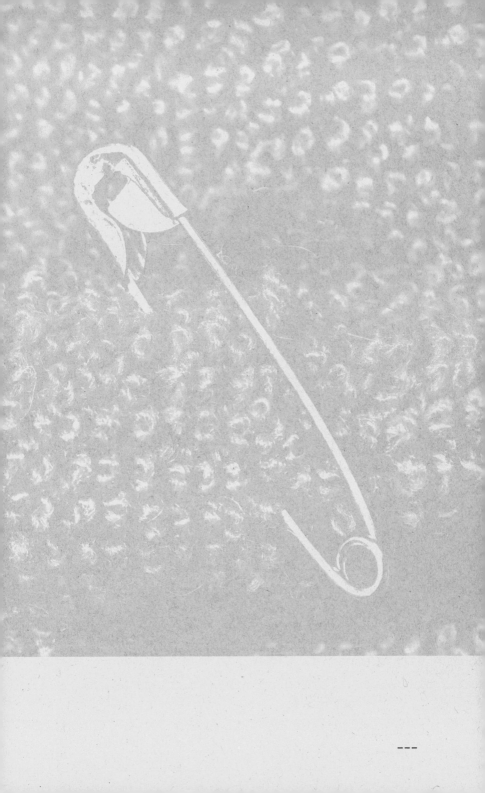

How to borrow from mythology: THE ROBIN HOOD TAX

The recklessness of the banking industry led to the
collapse of many of the world's largest economies.
Yet it wasn't long after they were bailed out
that many of the irresponsible practices and fat
bonuses returned.

Angered by this injustice, a group of activists
called for the introduction of a Tobin Tax.
This would place a small levy on all big payments
from one currency to another. A simple idea, but
with the potential to make the world economy a lot
more stable.

The problem was that the name Tobin Tax didn't sound
that interesting to anyone without an economics
degree. What they needed was an icon that people
could really understand and get behind.

A legendary character gave them their answer.
Symbolised as the Robin Hood Tax they had a simple
icon easily identified with - they were robbing
the rich to help the poor. Suddenly a complex fiscal
solution could be understood by anyone.

How to borrow from history: THE POPPY APPEAL

The First World War saw much of the French country-
side turn to fields of mud where little or nothing
could survive. All except the bright red Flanders
poppies, which somehow managed to grow in their
thousands, flourishing amid the chaos and destruction.

In the spring of 1915, shortly after losing his
friend in battle, Lt Col John McCrae was inspired by
the sight of the poppies to write his famous wartime
poem. His first couplet reads:

In Flanders fields the poppies blow
Between the crosses, row on row

Inspired by the poem, Moina Michael decided to make
a few silk poppies as an act of remembrance. Somehow
they came to the attention of the newly formed
Royal British Legion, who promptly ordered 9 million
of the flowers. They sold out on 11th November.

The Poppy Appeal has run every year since. During
the 100th anniversary of the war, 888,246 handmade
ceramic poppies were planted at the Tower of London.
Each represented a British and colonial soldier
who died in the Great War. The memorial was visited
by over 5 million people.

A_flexible_symbol_won't_get_bent_out_of_shape

Symbols help people show others that they belong.
It's why flags, T-shirts and badges have always been
a part of revolutions. They're the easiest way for
members to show their allegiance.

Today, that public display manifests itself in lots
of other ways. It could just as likely be a pinbadge,
a Twitter avatar or a black ink tattoo. So your
design needs to be simple and flexible enough to work
across all of them.

This means a standard shape. Thanks to social media,
your symbol needs to work in a relatively square
constraint, rather than being too tall or too long.

This means keeping colours clean. Unless you're
making it deliberately multicoloured, a symbol tends
to work best in one or two bold primary colours.

And this means making it replicable. The acid test is
whether others would be able to draw it on their own
placards by hand.

Look for symbolic actions

We've seen how rallying cries like Make Poverty History or Je Suis Charlie can become the identity of the revolution. But a great symbol can also become the way it's referred to.

This is especially true when that symbol represents your action in some way. The best feel strikingly novel. Whether that's growing a moustache or donning a red nose. If you've found a similarly original act to build your revolution around, make sure you put it front and centre as your defining icon.

There are no hard and fast rules as to what makes a successful action icon. More than anything, it simply relies on finding a powerful action to begin with. Something that isn't too hard or too expensive. Something rewarding for the person doing it. Something that takes you by surprise.

How making fun can trump making sense:
NAIL TRANSPHOBIA

Charlie Craggs wanted to do something about the
rising number of transgender hate crimes. She
knew that sitting down with a trans person
helped humanise the subject and put to bed any
misconceptions. She just needed an excuse to start
the conversation.

Her unlikely answer lay in nail art. Travelling
around the country with a pop-up salon, she invited
strangers in to get their nails done. Anyone
was welcome. And no questions were off limits.

And it was this action that gave Nail Transphobia
the perfect symbol, showing how Charlie was opening
hearts and minds one nail at a time.

<u>You can plan for the unexpected</u>

We're bombarded with thousands of logos and signs on a daily basis. And it's important that we inject some surprise into our symbol if we're to jolt people out of the image fatigue that can set in.

The first thing to go hunting for is irony. In a world of pristine white cleanliness, the paint splat of Dirt is Good stood out as a bold statement of intent. Combining similarly incongruous images can make for an equally memorable symbol.

Since many revolutions also deal with heavy issues, this can be a way to lighten the tone. The cheeky red noses stood out against the seriousness of fighting poverty. The vibrant pink saris of the Gulabi Gang were uplifting and optimistic, even though they were tackling domestic violence.

Never treat the cause flippantly or make light of the importance of the issue. But a surprising levity could provide the novelty it takes to pull people in.

How to think about what will get you noticed:
THE MOONWALK

When 13 women decided to power walk the New York
City Marathon for breast cancer awareness they
needed to generate some hype for their cause, whilst
also showing solidarity with those suffering from
the disease.

Their answer was their breasts themselves. Acting as
a symbol of female unity, they walked the marathon
in their bras. And duly raised the profile of their
fundraising efforts.

What started out as a one-off fundraising event
developed into Walk the Walk, a fully fledged
revolution. Their annual walks have raised over £99
million for vital breast cancer causes.

And the bras are no longer just an icon. They are the
springboard for many of their publicity drives too.
Fashion houses have designed limited editions,
celebrities have donated them and thousands of women
have customised their own with a dizzying array of
decoration that builds year on year.

Don't forget to colour it in

A strong colour can unify your followers. Just look
inside any football stadium on match day. But colour
can also provide your whole revolution with the
ability to be remembered.

There are various theories about the emotional cues
different colours provide. Whether it's the calm
of whites, the honesty of blues or the optimism
of yellows. Combinations can also be what makes
them distinctive. Think about the black and white
of Guinness and Newcastle United, or the rainbow
colourways of Pride and Google.

But a great colour is as much about its meaning as
it is about the aesthetics. And often you can take
inspiration from the issue. Livestrong was born
out of the famous yellow jersey Lance Armstrong
tended to be wearing at the time. The (RED) charity
built off the red already synonymous with the AIDS
awareness ribbon.

Whatever colours you arrive at, the important thing
is to commit. Great brands have always recognised
this. From red soft drinks to orange airlines to
blue social networks. They don't become restricted
by a distinctive palette. They use every piece of
communication as an opportunity to reinforce its
association with the brand.

How to know where you're not invited: LIVESTRONG

As they were designing the yellow supporter wristband for the Livestrong charity, Nike considered where their logo should go. In the end, they reached the right answer - nowhere.

Without the famous swoosh, wearers never felt their wrists were acting as free media for a multibillion pound company. They simply felt they were doing their bit to show support for fighting cancer.

The decision also helped get them onto the wrists of a huge number of high-profile celebrities who were unlikely to wear something branded.

The first invitation went out to the Cannes Film Festival with the words 'what are you wearing to Cannes?' Next came the Tour de France. Then the Olympics.

The wristbands became a conversation starter. Soon 75 million people wearing them became a chain of strength and unity. And despite their logo not being seen anywhere on the wristband, Nike were still credited with starting the revolution.

Make your symbol the spreadable variety

Revolutions aren't hierarchical. The most successful are those with a shared sense of ownership. And that democracy should extend to your symbol.

Encourage your followers to adopt your iconography for themselves and give them licence to play with it creatively as a meme. Such openness can quickly help spread its fame.

The distinctive font and layout of the Keep Calm and Carry On posters mean you always know what is being parodied. But it's simple enough for just about anyone to come up with their own version.

Try building from a simple template. Think about how you encourage its uptake as a meme. Give people scope for localisation.

All this will help it travel, but also work out what could stop it travelling. Avoid anything that's too complex, too clever or too cluttered as this will immediately put the brakes put on.

And if in doubt, check whether a six year old could draw it.

Get_by_with_a_little_help_from_your_friends

Great design is worth investing in. And great
designers want to create bold, impactful work. So
sell them on your vision for change. You'll be amazed
how much cheaper people are when they're excited by
the brief.

If cost is an issue, the good news is that there have
never been more talented designers to call on. Hunt
down students at the country's best design schools.
There's every chance you'll find someone itching
to get their work into the world. Or scour sites like
99designs.com and Behance and appeal to designers
you admire.

Whoever you brief, it's vital that they have a clear
sense of what you want to achieve. Talk them through
your fight, your action and your rallying cry. But
remember that the designer isn't there to solve any
confusion you might have.

Be as visual with your briefing as you can. Scour
Pinterest, Instagram and magazines. Use examples from
other brands or icons you like.

You should seek a symbol that's simple enough to be
adopted by others in whatever size and context they
see fit. But think beyond the icon itself. This is
an opportunity to establish the entire identity of
your revolution, so ask for a colour palette, fonts
and any elements of your existing identity that have
to be included.

```
--------------------------
```
Find your symbol

By exploring what your
    icon could mean
    (4A)
By exploring the tone
    (4B)

Find your symbol by exploring what your icon could mean

What is it?

Great symbols aren't about aesthetics, they're about
meaning. Looking good is simply a question of great
design, but becoming iconic requires your symbol to
build off something deeper.

How do I use it?

The first step is to come up with different angles.
So get sketching. Look to your rallying cry, look
for borrowed meaning you can steal and look at what
actions could be at the heart of your identity.
It doesn't matter if you can't draw; things can be
made to look pretty later.

HOW COULD YOUR SYMBOL ACT AS A CONVERSATION STARTER?

WHAT ACTION COULD PEOPLE TAKE THAT FUNCTIONS AS THE BASIS FOR YOUR SYMBOL?

HOW COULD YOUR SYMBOL TURN AN INVISIBLE ISSUE INTO SOMETHING MORE TANGIBLE?

COULD METAPHORS SYMBOLISE WHAT YOUR REVOLUTION SEEKS TO ACHIEVE?

WHAT EXISTING ICONOGRAPHY COULD YOU AMEND TO CREATE BORROWED MEANING FOR YOUR REVOLUTION?

WHAT ELEMENTS OF YOUR RALLYING CRY COULD BE REPRESENTED IN THE SYMBOL?

<u>Find your symbol by exploring the tone</u>

What is it?

Beyond the symbol itself, you also need to consider
the visual tone of your revolution. Imagery, colours
and type can all be combined to create a range of
different feelings.

How do I use it?

Start thinking about the attitude and spirit of
your revolution. Fill in the grid with imagery that
best represents how it should feel. Search online
or rip them out of magazines. None of these will be
simply copied, but they will provide useful clues
as to where the actual solution might lie.

Push your choices - you want as strong an identity
as you can find. And explain your decisions to the
designer so they can get closer to what you have in
your head. What was it that resonated? Why did you
pick one over another?

A COLOUR

A PIECE OF ART

A CELEBRITY

A LANDSCAPE

A FONT

AN ITEM OF
CLOTHING

<u>Before we move on... have you found your symbol?</u>

      The first test -
      Does it appeal?

We want the symbol to spread your revolution, whether
that's on placards, social networks or clothing. So
get a custom-made T-shirt with your symbol sat loud
and proud in the centre. Wear it for a day and see
how many people ask you about it. If that's too much,
share it on Instagram and see how many likes you get.

      The second test -
      Is it flexible?

Your revolution will be showing up in all manner of
places, but each will have its own different canvas.
Creating a symbol that's flexible enough to adapt
but distinctive enough to still be recognised is the
goal. Ask yourself whether it works as a silhouette.
Could you draw it on a dirty windscreen? Could you
stick it in a 2cm x 2cm square?

      The third test -
      Is it unique?

Remove the name from the symbol and show it to ten
people before asking who it reminds them of. If you
get the same response from more than three people
there's a chance that it is too closely associated
with something that already exists.

Notes

The Mindbomb

No matter how worthy your fight, unless you can get
the revolution in front of lots of people your impact
will always be limited.

This is the role of the mindbomb. It's the image
that's going to open the world's eyes, shock people
out of their indolence and lead them to act.
It's the image that will capture what's wrong in
an instant. It's the image that can't be ignored.

Not that it has to be a static image, of course. It
could be a viral film, a newsworthy stunt or a
hit song. The only requisite is that it gets people
talking and writing about your revolution so it
breaks out of the niches and into the mainstream.
And the good news is that this publicity is no longer
confined to the evening news or morning papers.

But mindbombs can still be the most daunting
challenge for a revolution. They demand creative
thinking and investment with no guarantee of success.

How do you get there? The answer is surprisingly
simple: you just have to ask whether your audience
will feel it. Emotion is what will make someone
take two minutes of their coffee break to watch your
film. What will make a journalist write about your
stunt over another story.

Your mindbomb needs to spoon-feed the facts and
force-feed the feeling. Because when you do, you'll
find out just how many people care enough to share.

<u>10 great mindbombs</u>

Dove's Real Beauty
Sketches viral film

The #OPTOUTSIDE store
closure for REI

Greenpeace's maiden anti-
whaling voyage

The movie An Inconvenient
Truth

Thich Quang Duc octo
himself on fire

Always' #LikeAGirl advert

Band Aid's Do they know
it's Christmas? single

Make Poverty History's
Click advert

Burger King's McWhopper
proposal to McDonalds

States United's Guns with
History viral film

An act is worth 1000 tweets

The Russian ship was bearing down on the exhausted
whale. Just as the harpoon flies into view, it
narrowly misses the two skinny hippies bobbing about
in a rubber boat. The photographer clicks his shutter
and the captured image is beamed around the world,
exposing millions to the brutality of the annual
whale hunt.

In many ways, this David and Goliath moment didn't
just launch Greenpeace - it launched the ecological
activist. With it, the concept of the mindbomb was
born. And since then many revolutions have forced
their way into people's minds thanks to a similarly
provocative action.

Not all mindbombs work in the same way. Some will
relate to a well-known cause, whereas others will
seek attention for an issue with very little public
awareness. There are mindbombs unlikely to provoke
much opposition because nobody disagrees with what
you stand for. And those where powerful enemies are
likely to oppose them.

The fight against whaling was already well known,
but the nations that supported it represented strong
opposition. Greenpeace's mindbomb had to shame this
group by turning it into a David vs Goliath battle.

For an issue like gay rights there is likely to be
far less opposition, but the challenge might be
getting people to connect with it by humanising the
story. Whilst for lesser-known fights it will be
about using evidence to either shock the world or
expose the opposition.

When you know your issue and know your enemy, you
know your story.

How_to_use_shock_to_reveal_the_truth:_THE_BOOK-
BURNING_PARTY

Following the financial crisis, local government cuts
were threatening to close the award-winning library
in the Michigan town of Troy. If a 0.7% tax increase
was not passed it would close.

Local residents fighting to keep the library open
knew such an increase represented a tiny amount
for most people. But mobilising the people of Troy
to vote in favour of a tax increase was still a
tough ask.

They needed to find something more emotive. Something
that people might just get angry about. So rather
than showing what people needed to give, they turned
the tables. And focussed on the books they were set
to lose.

They launched the novel idea of a book-burning party,
three days before the vote was due to take place.
In doing so, they reframed a vote for a tax rise
as a vote to burn books. And the 'Yes' vote to the
tax rise won by a landslide - 342% higher than
projections.

How to expose an issue with the evidence:
BACKWARD EVOLUTION

When Dove began their fight to make every woman
confident in her own beauty, they knew they
needed an enemy that would get people angry. And
they also needed the kind of damning evidence that
could indict them.

It was clear many women wanted to see images in
the media that were more representative of them.
Most women didn't look anything like the models
in the magazine.

More importantly, most of the models didn't look
anything like the models in the magazine. And this
was just the evidence they needed.

Dove made the viral film Backward Evolution to
show the lengths the fashion and beauty industry
went to manipulate the images we see every day.
The image of an airbrushed, photoshopped model is
reverse engineered to highlight the tricks that
are used to falsify beauty.

It was a wonderfully simple idea. And one quickly
picked up by the world's media to kickstart Dove's
revolution for real beauty.

How to connect by making it human: BULLY

Over 13 million American kids are bullied each year,
making it the most common form of violence experienced by young people. In fact, bullying has been an
issue ever since formal education began.

And that was just the problem. Bullying was often
seen as simply 'kids being kids' and this had allowed
it to become normalised.

The film Bully put the faces behind the statistics
in front of the world. Everyone knows what bullying
is, but far fewer people experience what it feels
like to be on the receiving end. These real, heart-
felt stories suddenly moved it from an issue you were
aware of into a pain you couldn't ignore.

It forced people to confront the issue. And made
America see that bullying is far from inevitable.
Over 500 cinemas showed the film and it was watched
by 2.5 million people.

How to shame by acting like David vs Goliath: BPGlobalPR

On the morning of May 19th 2010, Josh Simpson was watching a CBS reporter relay news of the Gulf of Mexico oil spill. Suddenly, the reporter was told by the Coast Guard to get off the beach or be arrested. When he protested that it was a public beach, he was simply told 'it's BP's rules'.

The incident planted the seed of a mindbomb in Josh's head. Creating a fake Twitter identity @BPGlobalPR, he started sending out messages about the oil spill. His parody was of an inept and insensitive public relations exec working for the company. And it hilariously scuppered BP's own attempts to control their message from behind a veil of anonymity.

It framed BP as the corporate monster picking on the everyman. A firm more worried about its own image than about what was actually happening. Within a week, @BPGlobalPR was twice as big as the official BP account itself.

When they began threatening to close the account down, Josh put out a tweet: 'I'm sorry you're upset. We're trying to make this right. Let us send you a free BP Cares T-shirt for $25 shipping.'

To his surprise, the requests came in. So he sent all the money to an environmental charity cleaning up the oceans. And this gave BP an even bigger headache: to close it down would be to stop someone raising money to help restore the Gulf.

Always remember that when it comes to David vs Goliath mindbombs, every move from your opponent is an opportunity for even more publicity.

NOBO
WILL
TO YOU
IF THE
NOTH
BY THE N

DY

ISTEN

LYRICS

'RE

OOKED

ELODY.

Lead the charge with emotion

John Medina is a molecular scientist who has spent
most of his life looking at how our brains process
stimuli. Successful mindbombs don't need an intimate
knowledge of the amygdala for success. But they do
need to know about emotion.

Emotion is what triggers dopamine, a neurotransmitter
that can be thought of as the brain's chemical
post-it notes. The more dopamine is triggered, the
more remembered the event. And the more emotion, the
more dopamine.

It's the reason people can remember specific details
about where they were during 9/11, such was the
strength of feeling at that moment. These events last
longer in our memories and with greater accuracy than
anything else.

Medina calls these emotionally charged events. But
we'll just call them a jaw-dropping moment. Something
that's so shocking, impressive or surprising that it
demands our attention and is remembered long after
the event itself.

It was only when every newspaper in the world showed
three year old Syrian refugee Aylan Kurdi washed
up on a Turkish beach that the world truly woke
up to the human cost of the refugee crisis. It was
horrific. But people began to act.

We need to apply the same principles to our
mindbombs. We're after films, headlines and images
that make people sit up. That shock. That pack
such an emotional punch that they can't be ignored.
Because only then will your revolution be remembered
and acted upon.

How to deliver an emotionally charged event:
MALARIA IS SPREAD BY MOSQUITOS

Bill Gates was halfway through his TED talk about
the threat millions face from malaria each year.
Then he produced a glass jar.

"Malaria is spread by mosquitos. I brought some
here. I'll let them roam around. There is no reason
only poor people should have the experience."

With that, Gates released a swarm of mosquitoes
into the auditorium. Of course, the insects
weren't infected. But he'd made his point: why
should we be blessed with good fortune?

He'd done it more effectively by creating an
experience rather than simply lecturing people.
It was a jaw-dropping moment, an emotionally
charged event.

And it helped him create a media swarm far bigger
than the mosquitos flying around the room. A
Google search provides over half a million stories
on the event.

Get mad and you might get even

Despite the tension between the Western Allies and
the Soviet Union during World War II, they shared a
common enemy. And that was all they needed to work
together. As Churchill said, 'if Hitler invaded hell,
I would make at least a favourable reference to the
Devil in the House of Commons'.

In other words, the enemy of your enemy can be your
friend. And whilst revolutions can rise and spread
without belief in God, it's rare they do so without
belief in a Devil. A shared nemesis can create
an outrage that stretches across your followers'
backgrounds or beliefs. Just ask Mods (or Rockers),
Liverpool fans (or Man Utd ones), Republicans (or
Democrats).

Just as in any good movie, the best villains are more
memorable than the heroes. They might be unrepentant.
They might be the good guy turned bad. Or they might
enjoy a charisma we simply love to hate.

Tabloid newspaper editors will tell you that their
front pages need to deliver either shame or anger.
So your enemy doesn't have to be the one who's most
to blame. They have to be the one that gets people
most angry.

Outrage is important because it acts as a passion
trigger. The brain and heart start working together.
Caring turns into hating. And hating turns wouldn't
it be nice into when will it change?

How to make our indolence the enemy: FUCK THE POOR

The Pilion Trust was one of many charities threatened
by a 20% decline in donations and a 60% decline in
government funding. And they needed £50,000 to keep
their homeless shelter open.

They knew that people still cared about homelessness
and the work they did. But charities can't survive on
good intentions alone; they need donations.

So they turned to a mindbomb. A hidden camera filmed
a campaigner with a sandwich board reading 'FUCK THE
POOR'. Not surprisingly, he was on the receiving end
of abuse from dozens of offended passers-by.

But when the same man carries a 'HELP THE POOR' board
moments later, people simply walk past.

The contrast showed that no matter how much we might
say we care, the most important thing is to act.
Nobody wants to be seen as a 'poor-hater' yet most of
us pass up the opportunity to help whenever we can.

Through highlighting these hypocritical attitudes
towards poverty in such an entertaining way, the film
helped donations increase 1,600% and the Pilion Trust
met their target three times over. All with just £500
and a piece of cardboard.

ASSUM

WILL G

DAMN.

WORSHI

TEMPLE

P

UNTIL P

BE I

NO-ONE

A

HEN

AT THE

OF

BLICITY

OU CAN'T

VORED.

Laugh at your enemy's expense

Once you take music videos out of the equation, the 10 most watched YouTube films of all time attract their audience through humour. And when you tackle a serious issue with a dose of mischief it can provide an incongruity that gets noticed.

As with any mindbomb, the key with humour is to provoke. All great comedy has a fall guy, and when you mock your enemy it can also help to show the folly of their ways.

Look at how Sarah Silverman's Great Schlep used political parody to mock Republican voters and convince young Jewish voters to root for Obama. Or how the generosity of giving away free croissants during the EU Referendum put the spotlight on the Leave campaign's increasingly threatening tactics.

Try spoofs, try sketches, try satire. Do the unexpected, the extreme, maybe even the risky. You'll certainly have a much better chance of getting people's attention.

How to make parody your most powerful weapon:
KIDS VS FASHION

Yolanda Dominguez was increasingly concerned by
the imagery fashion brands used to launch their
annual campaigns. And specifically what the photos
said about women's role in society versus men's.

To make her point, she turned to a group of 8 year
olds and simply asked them to describe what they
saw in the photos.

Their candid answers were striking. They saw the
women as drunk, ill and lonely. Sad individuals
in need of help. Men on the other hand were
heroes and bosses, happy and strong. Women were
subservient, whereas men were in control.

The children then adopted the ludicrous poses
they'd seen in many of the models, parodying the
highfalutin world of high-end fashion.

The way kids decoded the images and blew wide open
the implicit violence and inequality was a much
more powerful statement than Yolanda could ever
make herself. Whilst their answers helped lighten
the tone in a way that only children can.

One man's loss can be your gain

In economics, loss aversion describes people's
tendency to prefer avoiding losses to acquiring
gains. It explains why losing a £10 note feels worse
than finding one feels good. Studies suggest
that, psychologically, losses are twice as powerful
as gains.

It's a phenomenon that has been used by the insurance
industry for years. But we can also use it for
our mindbombs. Think of it as identity aversion;
the desire to not be seen as a bad person is more
powerful than the motivation to be seen as good.

The LGBT movement has long known this. Many people
are compelled by the promise of equal rights for
all, but there are just as many who simply don't want
to be labelled a bigot. Even if they're not staunchly
pro-gay, they certainly don't want to be seen as
the enemy.

So ask yourself, what would people who didn't support
your revolution be? Narrow-minded, thoughtless,
delusional? Mercenary, selfish or even guilty? Find
the opposite identity to the one your followers would
want and create some noise around that.

How one image can tell your story: #MOREWOMEN

Women are noticeably absent from many prominent parts
of public life. Whether that's comedy panel shows
or the benches of Westminster. Everyone knows it, but
very few do anything about it.

Which is why Elle magazine started their #MoreWomen
campaign fighting for more women sitting around
society's top tables.

And their mindbomb played with this in a very
literal sense. A series of images simply showed what
governments, committees and TV shows around the
world would look like if the men were photoshopped
out. They were practically empty.

The magazine made a striking video to accompany the
campaign but it was the simple images that were most
powerful. When your picture can save them writing
1000 words, journalists the world over will be more
than willing to copy and paste your publicity.

WRIT
SOMET

READ
DO SON
WORTH
TWE

ING
WORTH
NG OR
THING

TING.

Take time to investigate

It's been said that stories are just data with a soul.
And as media organisations slash their investigative
budgets, there is an opportunity for revolutions to
step in and expose to the world the issues it needs
to see.

The more surprising the evidence you can find, the
better. No More Page 3 discovered that many companies
targeting young girls advertised in The Sun newspaper.
One of these was Lego, so they drove a huge topless
Lego model straight to their theme park. The point was
simple: if you care about young girls' imaginations,
stop funding the paper that is doing more than most to
damage them.

You may even be able to turn your investigation into
a documentary that acts as your mindbomb. The End
of the Line revealed how overfishing was threatening
bluefin tuna stocks. As a result, Marks & Spencer
switched to more sustainable skipjack tuna for
the 20,000 sandwiches it sold every day. And this was
used to challenge other retailers to do the same.

Asking why somebody isn't supporting the revolution
can be a powerful tactic. Especially if the reason is
their own financial gain. So follow the money trail:

1.   List the sources of revenue for your enemy, or
        whoever stands in the way of change.

2.   Embark on a focussed campaign against a few
        key supporters, rather than the blanket
        approach. You can always broaden your efforts
        later.

3.   Ask them specific questions. Don't just talk
     about their financial support, but find out
     all the specific ways they support your enemy.

4.   Consider whether publicity can be generated to
     put them in the spotlight. Can you play with
     their own identity, logos or products to mock
     them in some way?

5.   Be persistent. Don't be put off by meaningless
     PR-speak.

Your revolution is your story

Startling facts can be great for a short-term
spike in interest, but people tend to quickly forget
them. The good news is that they rarely forget
startling fables.

Stories have been our way of communicating for
millennia and our brains are now hardwired to process
information using a few basic narratives. A great
story suspends our disbelief, so our audience is
less likely to get bogged down in the nitty-gritty
of the argument.

But stories are not just more memorable and more
persuasive. They are also more effective.

Until recently, emotion has been thought of as a
hindrance to decision-making. The reason we shouldn't
let our hearts rule our head. But neuroscientists
have found that the frontal lobes, where our decision
-making happens, are actually triggered by emotions
rather than facts.

In other words, without emotions we can't even make
decisions. And when we tell stories that make our
audience feel something, it's much more likely
that they will go on to act on it. Whether that's
donating money, changing their behaviour or simply
signing a petition.

So you need to turn your revolution into its very
own story. Getting there shouldn't be too tricky
because all great stories are journeys of change.

You simply need to take the thing you're fighting
to change and apply some well-worn narrative techniques to add some drama:

Goals, stakes and urgency

All stories are built around a goal. In your case
this is the change you want to see in the world.
But thinking about what is at stake if things don't
change can often provide a more gripping narrative.
Dove might fight to change the beauty industry but
they focus on the self-esteem of women. Then see
if you can find a ticking timebomb that gives that
quest real urgency.

Show, don't tell

This old adage applies to just about any storytelling medium. Simply make sure your audience is
experiencing the story through actions, thoughts
and demonstrations rather than lengthy explanations
and description.

Make 'em feel

Everyone has a heart. And the things that touch
it are the same the world over. As Wilkie Collins
said: 'make 'em cry, make 'em laugh, make 'em
wait'. Think about how many of these often carry
a physical reaction too. Your stories need to
provide goosebumps, tears and bellyaching laughs.

A PRICE
IDEA CA
NOTHIN
YOU ME
CREA
YOUR

EUS

COST

WHEN

VITY.

RRENCY.

The_revolution_will_not_be_televised

Social video is a potent tool for any revolution. It doesn't judge your production or media spend, simply whether your film deserves to be famous. Great ones can travel fast. They can travel far. And they can travel more cheaply than ever before. But remember that OK video doesn't get liked and average stories don't get shared.

1.   Hit them with emotion

You're after a physical reaction - laughter, tears, repulsion, shock, surprise.

2.   Turn the volume up to 11

Quite funny or quite interesting won't cut it. You need to be extreme. Act decisively and courageously.

3.   Start strong

40% of all social activity is in the first three days, peaking on day two. So when you press go, make sure you're ready to capitalise on this.

4.   Let it go

Let people comment, download, embed, and shorten your content.

5.   Kickstart the sharing

The biggest viral successes tend to insure their success through paid distribution or significant social campaigns that encourage people to pass them on.

<u>Help is at hand</u>

The iconic Obama Hope image began as 350 posters sold
on the street by Shepard Fairey. And if you have
a fight that others believe in, there's every chance
you'll find creative people willing to lend their
support too.

So draw up a list of anyone you think could help:

-    Scout around Behance.com for designers who've
     worked with causes before - many creative
     people are keen to use good as an outlet for
     their work.

-    Speak to artists to see if they can produce
     limited edition works.

-    See if your favourite YouTube stars will come
     up with video ideas.

-    Contact comedy writers for sketches.

-    Ask musicians to write a campaign song.

-    Contact film producers to see if they'd be
     interested in taking an open brief.

There remains one sentence that will always get ideas
people interested: 'I'm going to give you complete
creative freedom'. The better the brief, the
more time people will devote to it. The less they'll
expect to be paid. And the more they will care.

How to get others on board: PROMISED LAND

Writers Adam Reynolds and Chaz Harris noticed that
the role models children are presented with tend to
be very stereotyped and very straight.

They wanted a mindbomb that could start to change
that. As writers they couldn't help notice how so
many fairy tales were about romance but didn't
include examples of modern love or different family
structures.

So they wrote Promised Land, a children's book
where a young prince and a young farm boy fall in
love - with each other. But of course, the very
best children's books are loved as much for their
illustrations as the prose.

So they launched a Kickstarter campaign. And when
illustrator Christine Luiten heard about the project
she was happy to lend her help. Together they
produced a book that charmed readers as much as it
challenged norms.

Tactics_trump_strategy

You want to blow the world away with your mindbomb.
But because so much of its success relies on
word of mouth, it might just take an unexpected big
news story that day to deny you the viral storm
you deserve.

So arm yourself with cluster bombs. Think in terms
of a series of publicity plays rather than just
one. Richard Curtis said that Make Poverty History
'wasn't one big launch, but a constant series
of relaunches. We'd do one thing, and if that didn't
work, we'd try another'.

It's always better to get something done rather than
planning endlessly for an event that never happens.
Don't agonise for weeks about doing exactly the
right thing; just do what you think is most right.
Live life in beta. Constantly testing and learning as
you go. Sure, you'll fail sometimes. But you'll fail
faster, and move onto growing your successes quicker.

Get into the habit of developing ideas on a regular
basis. Make it a ritual. And make it everyone's
responsibility. Even if you think you have more
activities than you need, there may come a point when
you don't. Ideas bring momentum to the revolution.
They ensure you never run out of fuel.

WHEN
WI

IS SIL
NOT
LOUD

Cl

Never forget number one

You have a passion that pulled you into this fight
to begin with. It's important to remember that
people will respond to that. So don't be afraid to
speak directly to the camera. Look your audience in
the eyes. And give them a glimpse of your soul.

What would be your best pitch? An Inconvenient
Truth was just PowerPoint and a DSLR but it was
simple, evocative and terrifying. What's your best
lecture? Watch Ken Robinson or Jamie Oliver or
Pam Warhurst on TED. You need to treat these people
as your opposition. Learn from them.

One of the most compelling things can be simply
speaking from the heart. Read your manifesto out on
YouTube. If it comes naturally, be funny. Tell the
world of your struggle. Be humble. Be vulnerable.
But most importantly, be real. People will be drawn
to your authenticity.

```
--------------------------
Find your mindbombs

By understanding what
    needs to happen
    (5A)
By tapping into different
    emotions
    (5B)
```

Find your mindbombs by understanding what needs to happen

What is it?

All mindbombs need to create awareness but certain
tactics can be more effective at doing this,
depending on the nature of what's being tackled.

How do I use it?

Ask whether you are taking on a well-known issue
or an unknown one. Then consider whether this is
something that people are likely to accept, or
if there is likely to be opposition. This will tell
you what your mindbomb needs to do.

But remember that there are shocking David vs
Goliath tales. And you can expose an issue by
humanising it. This is less about the tone of your
mindbomb and more about what it needs to achieve.

LITTLE OPPOSITION—
PROVOKE YOUR AUDIENCE

UNKNOWN ISSUE

KNOWN ISSUE

SHOCK BY
REVEALING
THE TRUTH

CONNECT BY
HUMANISING
THE ISSUE

EXPOSE BY
INVESTIGATING
THE EVIDENCE

SHAME BY
TURNING IT
INTO DAVID
VS GOLIATH

STRONG OPPOSITION —
PROVOKE YOUR ENEMY

<u>Find your mindbomb by tapping into different emotions</u>

What is it?

The success of your mindbomb will depend on what you
make people feel. It rests on whether you can move
them or entertain them.

How do I use it?

Explore how you could provoke a series of emotions.
Start by taking the emotion you're naturally drawn
towards and come up with three ideas that could
trigger that.

Then do the same for a feeling you never thought
you'd use. An unexpected emotion may offer the best
chance of standing out. The more extreme the
reaction, the greater the chance you have of lodging
your revolution in the collective conscience of
the world.

ENTERTAIN PEOPLE
MAKE ME MARVEL
MAKE ME SURPRISED
MAKE ME LAUGH
MAKE ME CURIOUS
WHAT DO YOU FEEL?
MAKE ME GRATEFUL
MAKE ME ANGRY
MAKE ME CARE
MAKE ME CRY
MOVE PEOPLE

<u>Before we move on... have you found your symbol?</u>

       The first test -
       Does it provoke an emotion?

The most reliable way of getting someone's attention
is to make them feel. You need to be aiming for
split sides and goosebumps, deep breaths and
damp eyes. Because when you create an emotional
reaction in someone they won't just keep it to themselves; they'll share it with others. Look for the
Marmite effect - do they love it or hate it? It
often doesn't matter which. You just need to avoid
everything in between.

       The second test -
       Is it arresting?

Your mindbomb needs to create a noise you can't miss,
for a revolution nobody's heard of. This might be
bringing an unknown issue to the world's attention,
or it might require a new take on something we've
grown apathetic about. It just needs to make people
sit up. The words to listen out for are 'I didn't
expect that'.

       The third test -
       Is it worth sharing?

Your mindbomb relies on others spreading fame for
you. But journalists have never had more sources
for their stories, and everyone has increasingly
cluttered social streams. So you need to challenge
yourself. Will a journalist really write about
this? Will a Facebook user really like it? Make fame
your metric.

Notes

The Propaganda

No matter how loudly you've launched your revolution, people quickly move on. Without a sizeable media budget to buy more noise, you'll need to think creatively about how to achieve a constant hum in popular culture.

There have never been more opportunities. New media networks like Facebook and Buzzfeed actively rely on compelling content for their success. Armed with a mobile phone, the savvy revolutionary has all the media buys they need in their pocket.

But whilst your messages can quickly and cheaply reach a global audience, you're also up against an ever-higher mountain of content. Your news needs to sit at the top.

This means going native. Look to ape the type of content that finds success in each platform. Add to people's experience, don't detract from it.

This means being generous. Spend more time inspiring than interrupting.

And this means being human. Be interested in the things your audience are interested in and understand when to be quiet.

Do this and you'll find a host of cost effective ways to spread your propaganda. Often, all they'll cost is the price of an idea.

10 great opportunities for propaganda

Calendar events -
From Back to School to
Talk Like a Pirate Day

Think Tank reports -
Act like a real person
by having a POV on
what others are saying

Prophetic wisdom -
Moving messages
beautifully presented
are the crack cocaine
of social sharing

Images -
Perhaps the easiest way
to spread through the
internet quickly, and
a technique to apply to
all your propaganda

Awards -
Celebrate your heroes
and your villains;
people are always
keen to know life's
winners and losers

Retweets -
Be generous with your
own sharing. Find
friends and show
support for others and
they will help you

Research -
Give journalists
everywhere some new and
surprising stats and
you've done half their
job for them

Lists -
The internet loves a
new top 10. Serve up
some of your content
in a new format

Celebrity quotes -
Whether it's the Pope
or Kanye West, there
are people with strong
opinions out there
who you can respond to
and comment on

Popular culture -
Use what people are
tweeting and talking
about already. Offer
a new perspective.
Play with the content.
Parody it. Then share
it with the world

<u>Get jabbing</u>

It's tempting to think that your social media
strategy will deliver a knockout punch. But in
boxing you shouldn't overlook the value of ground
work. Think of your propaganda as round after
round of jabs that work away at the target to
maximise your chance of victory.

Great storytellers have always known this. Dickens
initially published all of his work in weekly
newspapers and journals. He needed to create a
series of dramatic events to get his readers back
week after week. And so should you.

Consider jabs as the sparring that keeps your
audience curious along the journey. New stories,
fresh ideas, content, opinion pieces. The climactic
right hook will come too, but it will have far less
meaning without the exposition that comes before it.

A constant stream of fresh content is no guarantee
of success. You need to pay close attention to all
the variables that can influence its effectiveness -
the time you posted, whether you used a hashtag, how
people respond to a photo versus an animated GIF.
And the dozens of other factors you can play with.

Your social media efforts will require both quantity
and quality. Just like your boxing, they will only
improve through practice and observation.

<u>Fan the flames of popular culture</u>

It can often be easier to pour petrol on an existing
fire than to always start one from scratch yourself.
And every day the world presents sparks for you to
build publicity around.

You'll find these sparks in the culture that
surrounds you. They're in blogs, in magazines and in
the free paper on your way into work. They're sitting
behind every Twitter refresh. And they're on those
websites like BuzzFeed, Mashable and PSFK which
increasingly represent the world's cultural pulse.

Be alert to the opportunities all this content
provides. Get into the habit of digesting it on a
daily basis. Subscribe to the best newsletters. Set
up Google alerts around fertile topics. And only
follow people on Twitter and Medium that actually
deliver new news.

Most of all, remember that these sparks still require
that petrol to be poured on them. You might fan the
flames with spoof and parody. You might get angry.
You might offer a disruptive point of view. Whatever
you do needs to provoke that same emotional reaction
as your mindbomb, so that people are more likely to
share it.

And never underestimate the importance of small
delivered often. Those flickering flames can quickly
turn into a blaze.

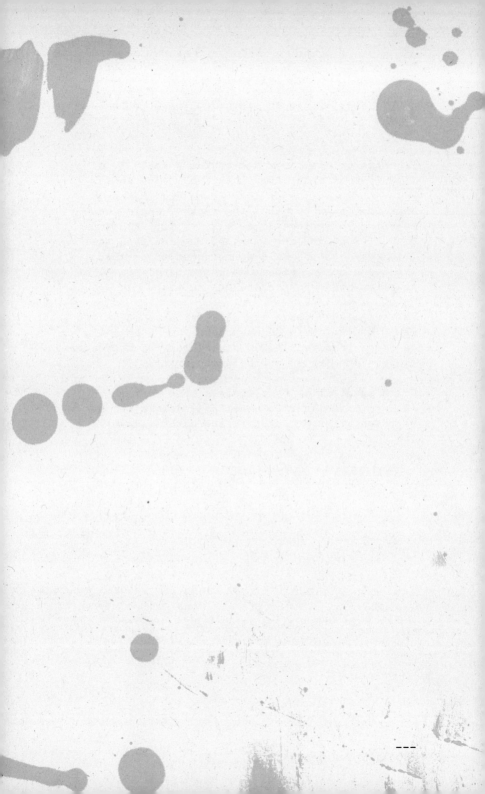

Caroline Criado-Perez set up The Women's Room to fight female underrepresentation in the media.

When she found out that the Bank of England was planning to replace Elizabeth Fry with Winston Churchill on the new £5 note, she realised that this meant there would be no women other than the Queen on our cash. She'd found her spark, and duly set about pouring petrol on it.

The campaign to have the Bank put a woman on the new £10 note was a huge success. Her change.org petition received 36,000 signatures and they agreed to put Jane Austen on the notes from 2017.

Most importantly, Caroline was able to turn one small tactic into a national debate on the representation of women in the establishment.

Plan to be spontaneous

You don't always have to build momentum around your revolution from scratch when there are plenty of established events you can use to your advantage. You just need to plan in advance.

Retailers know the importance of Christmas and plan for it every year in this way. But there are dozens of other dates that come round every year – public holidays, sporting events, awards shows, International Days of the X, Y and Z. All of these are potential sparks.

The challenge is to find an interesting way of using them. Think laterally. If you are fighting for affordable lighting for schoolchildren in rural Africa, you could draw attention to this on December 21st, the darkest day of the year.

Or it might be less of an annual event and more of a moment in time. Make Poverty History knew that 2005 could be a monumental year in the fight against world poverty: the UK was hosting both the G8 world leaders and the presidency of the European Union. So throughout the year there was a series of preplanned events that the revolution could build news around.

Think about what's happening in the world. Whether that's the Olympics, the turn of the decade or annual themes from the UN. All represent potential fuel for your propaganda.

TEREUT

VEED

NTEREST

S.

Lies, damned lies and statistics

One of PR's oldest tricks is creating a compelling statistic. Numbers have the benefit of showing, not telling. They can make the case for your revolution unequivocal and easily understood. There are a few tricks you can use to find more interesting ones:

Currency conversion

Journalists and readers respond to novelty. So this might require re-expressing your statistics as a different, more surprising metric. For instance, the number of deaths from malaria each year is the equivalent to losing the entire populations of Manchester and Edinburgh.

Times table

If the statistic doesn't feel particularly compelling in its own right, could it be represented in a way that gives it more oomph? Oxfam found that the richest 62 people in the world were as wealthy as half the world's population. Look at the cumulative value. Ask what your data might mean over several years. Try to work out what it represents as the proportion of something else.

And the survey says...

Journalists thrive on data, so make life easier for them. A survey can provide a new finding that gives them something tangible to use. And it's never been

easier to gauge people's opinions - sites like Google
Consumer Surveys, Typeform and SurveyMonkey help you
set something up in minutes.

Make it meaningful

Readers like to know what it means for them, so
create metrics in tangible terms. Many women have to
walk over six miles for water each day. But the fact
that this is further each day than the average UK car
travels makes that fact come alive.

Make it sing

When you do find a great stat, help them stand
out. Create infographics that people will share.
Take a look at www.silk.co. It will help turn your
interesting numbers into visualisations with even
more impact.

Think like an editor

Amongst all the creative ways of gaining buzz, it can be easy to overlook something as arcane as the humble press release. But releasing news updates in this way still acts as a sign that you're serious and professional.

Success relies on getting into the heads of editors. Even if they are interested in your issue, they don't want to comb through pages of prose trying to decipher what you're actually doing and why.

Start by writing well. Distil why your revolution exists into something clear and digestible. Make it conversational. Keep it succinct and to the point. And don't forget to include your contact details.

Consider how bullet points can help you be more succinct. What are five reasons this has to stop? What's your 10-point plan? The three things you want to see changed?

And remember that journalists and their readers thrive on novelty. Being the first, the biggest or the most anything piques their interest. So challenge yourself. Get into the habit of only ever writing 'the world's first...' press releases.

FASTER

TYOURR

MISTAKES

VE YOU

~~RKWURD~~

~~OREWARD~~

ORWARD

Work out how long you have

So where do all these jabs take place? This
propaganda needs to sit somewhere and you'll find a
whole range of social channels perfect for storing
and sharing your news.

But each platform requires a different formula.
What works on Facebook might not be so effective on
Twitter. Copying and pasting the same content into
every social channel won't work; you need to think
about how you can make it native to each environment.

Your content should reflect the reason the user went
to that platform to begin with. Mimic the aesthetics,
the tone, the function. If it's primarily an
entertainment network, you need to entertain them.
If people are there for news, give them news.

In doing this, you may find that you get more
traction on certain platforms. Your revolution might
shine within the beauty pageant on Instagram, or
win the comedy stakes on Twitter. It's often
more effective to be amazing somewhere rather than
OK everywhere.

<u>Instagram_and_Pinterest:_where_you_have_1_second_to
be_aspirational</u>

For now, pictures rule the social world. People use
photos as their emotional wish list. They tell the
world who you are, or who you want to be. Images
reflect ideals. And you have to make your revolution
another one.

Witty and prophetic placards have accompanied many of
the world's most famous revolutions. These placards
are now just as likely to be found online. Go back to
your rallying cry and see what other mantras could be
used. Then turn to the three rules of sharing.

First, deliver eye candy. The most gorgeous,
arresting imagery rises to the top. Pimp your shots
with slow-mo, time lapse and editing apps.

Second, express yourself authentically. Popular
instagrammers tend to follow a particular theme and
enjoy a signature look. Users are drawn to images
with an element of craft, so stay away from anything
that feels like you're advertising. And never steal.

Finally, get your images out there. Turbo-charge them
with a great caption, using tags and links as the
gateway through which others will discover your
content. Go for quality over quantity on the hashtags,
and avoid any 'tags for likes' tactics.

<u>Twitter: where you have 2 seconds to be part
of a trend</u>

Twitter's main currency is news and information,
delivered within 140 characters and the odd photo
or short video. Think of it as the pulse of the
internet. The ability of your followers to retweet
these updates amongst many followers means that
they can soon find a large audience if they are
compelling enough to share.

It's tempting to treat Twitter as an announcement
medium or a link to bulkier content on your blog.
But neither of these tactics is likely to lead to
retweets. Without careful thought your tweets will
be tiny drops in the ocean of updates that hits
people whenever they head to the site.

You're likely to enjoy more success bringing a fresh
spin on something that's already created interest.
Especially if that spin is provocative or funny.
You're after OMGs and LOLs.

The trending function will tell you where to start
fishing. Keep an eye on memes, words and phrases
that have gone viral. All of these represent low-
hanging fruit if you can remix them in a way that
relates to your revolution.

And if you do want to use your followers to create
your own trend, make sure you put the new into
their newsfeed. In that sea of sameness, it's only
the wittiest lines, the most poignant anecdotes
and the boldest assertions that stand any chance
of travelling.

Facebook: Where you have 3 seconds to update the
community

The tweets you put out will be useful, but Twitter
is a busy place. When it comes to hosting your
content and creating a community, turn to Facebook.

This is where people go to connect, to socialise and
to catch up on what their friends are doing. So when
you make your revolution become one of these friends,
that's exactly what you need to provide.

It might be a more benign audience, but you still
need to take the same care and attention with your
updates. Research suggests that as more and more
updates are read on mobiles, you have three seconds
before your audience's fingers will start scrolling.

So ensure that your text isn't too long. Use a
simple call to action that doesn't ask too much of
the audience. Don't speak too often.

And most importantly, ask whether what you're putting
out there is actually going to interest anyone. Make
sure what's on your mind makes your supporters feel
proud, angry or surprised.

<u>YouTube: where you have 10 seconds to hook them with
your story</u>

Video isn't the future of the internet. It's the here
and now. As content, it enjoys more views and deeper
engagement than just about any of its peers. But
it will take less than 10 seconds of watching for the
viewer to decide whether they're going to give you
any more time or switch off.

This means signposting early on what the viewer
is going to be rewarded with for their time. Think
about the way the first 10 minutes of movies tee
up the next 90. They set the tone and the moral and
establish what you'll get if you hang around until
the end. Is there a cliffhanger you can use early on
to keep people for the next 90 seconds?

Remember, you're not just giving them 30 frames a
second. You're giving them a story. Something that
they can relate to or escape to. Make sure your video
provides one of the two. It will need big emotions
or big excitement.

And once you have a success on your hands, make sure
you capitalise on it. Quickly create more great
videos to turn it into a series rather than a stunt.
Consider what your magic formula is. It could be
the format, the presenter or even the scheduling.
People enjoy the same repetition and familiarity in
their YouTube content as they do in their TV shows.

This will still build a steady following even if
none of the follow-up videos hit the heights of your
first success. YouTube isn't just a host for your
video content, it's a social network too. Learn how
to use cards, links and annotations within the films
themselves so you can build your following and
encourage sharing.

Medium, BuzzFeed and blogging: where you have 60 seconds to make an argument

Longer-form written content might not enjoy the scale of video or the immediacy of images but it is a medium inherently suited to revolutions. Words are still a great way to make an argument. Find the right context and you'll find the keyboard is mightier than the sword.

Medium doesn't have same scale as many other networks, but its content often carries more thought. Designed as the home for ideas that change the world, it is the most journalistic of the platforms.

So go back to why you began this revolution to begin with. Remember why things need to change. Open your audience's eyes to issues they haven't thought about yet. Deliver an analysis that's insightful, passionate and moving.

And when you've done all that, turn that article into a listicle and head to the community section of BuzzFeed. This platform is fast emerging as the way millions of young people digest the news. They go there for succinct arguments rather than feature-length editorial. So how can you turn your propaganda into a quick list that someone could read and share whilst they're waiting for their flat white?

The advantage Medium and BuzzFeed have is their reach; you needn't just rely on others coming to you. But if you can direct readers from them and onto your own blog as well, you'll be able to win them over with even more of your content and encourage them to sign up as an ally.

Snapchat and Instagram Stories: where you have 24 hrs to show them behind the scenes

Snapchat is a mobile only network and is sometimes difficult to get your head around. On the face of it, content looks cheap, doesn't last and is hard to find. But it's precisely because Snapchat removes the veneer of many other networks that users come to trust and enjoy it.

The thing that marks this content out is the fact it is disposable. The platform spread through Messages, where you can send photo and video content to your contact list and set how long they can be viewed for.

Today you're more likely to find the Stories feature useful. Snack size video is broadcast as a series of moments, building up to tell the story of a particular day, event or moment. They're available to all your friends for a 24-hour period.

This makes it great for giving people an insider's look behind the scenes of the revolution. The stories act as windows into a select world and are only likely to be discovered by your most ardent supporters.

You'll find authenticity is crucial. The platform is built on immediacy and unpolished imagery. That's what users love, so don't get too hung up on the production values. Videos are shot directly on a smartphone in selfie-mode to give a lo-fi, warts-and-all type of content.

One final challenge is that there's no profile bio, custom photo or link to your site. So unless people are looking it's unlikely they'll find you. Ensure you make it easier for them by promoting your username and creating a 'ghost' Snapcode image so that your audience can use their cameras to find you more easily.

Deliver tomorrow today

This is a glimpse of the tools available today. But
you'll find the fight is easier with the most up-to-
date weaponry. And as the tools to create great
film continue to become cheaper and simpler, video
is likely to be central to many of the networks
of tomorrow.

That video might be shorter. Platforms like Instagram
stories and Snapchat encourage mini-stories through
clever editing.

That video might be faster. Facebook Live and
Periscope turn anyone into a broadcaster. Now your
supporters can follow that stunt or event as
it happens.

That video might be wider. 360 and augmented reality
are starting to provide a rich canvas to play with.
The New York Times used it to tell the stories of
three of the 30m refugee children displaced by war.

Or that video might be more narrow. With more of our
audience on phone screens, we'll have to learn how
to shoot great portrait video too. Platforms like
Musical.ly are helping us along the way.

Of course, that video might not be video. It could
be something we can't yet conceive of, being put
together in a Stanford garage right now. But the
advantage of the newest platforms will always be that
the early adopters tend to skew young. And that's
precisely the same demographic most likely to get
involved in campaigning for social change.

ONLY O
TO WH
ANYTHIN
EVER
· ISN

OMMIT

MATTERS.

IS POSSIBLE.

HING.

Don't throw out the old when you're in with the new

With this array of options, it can be easy to forget something as humble as an email. Signing subscribers up to a simple newsletter can grow your community and grow your brand. But don't be blinded by their apparent simplicity. Before you add a newsletter to your digital toolbox make sure you know how to use it properly:

Reward your inner circle

These are your most loyal followers. Reward that with privilege by making them the first to hear your news and see your content. Tell them what you've been up to, your successes and breakthroughs.

Don't be afraid to ask for help

Whatever the request may be, your subscribers are probably the most willing. Get people to watch one of your videos, share an article or sign up their friends.

But it's not all about you

Resist the temptation to just fire requests, though. Sandwich them between interesting content you curate from around the web. Entertainment, updates and guest posts. This is the content that will keep the invitation to their inbox open.

Focus on content, not design

Instead of wasting time on fancy graphics, use it to find a repeatable format. NextDraft has become one of the most subscribed newsletters by focussing on 10

things you need to know each day. Keep things simple.
Keep them interesting.

Develop your timing and rhythm

Build a schedule that you can stick to and your
readers will appreciate your rhythm. Once a week, the
first Monday of the month, whatever works for you and
your stats.

Give it your personality

Don't slip into an announcement voice. Try to make
it about you.

Leave the leg work to others

Managing this can be daunting. But services such as
Mailchimp are simple to use and free for up to 2000
subscribers.

Sign 'em up

Use a polite opt-in pop-up on your site. Promote a
sign-up page. Adopt a forward-to-a-friend button on
your updates.

Mix it up

Test all the variables to see what's most effective.
Subject lines, numbers of articles, scheduling. And
be in it for the long haul.

<u>Your world wide hub</u>

Your revolution should always be moving, responding
to opportunity and creating news. Your Facebook
community will be one home for these, but many
people will also be looking for a website. Let
WordPress or Squarespace do the donkeywork for you.
Their templates can provide the perfect place for:

-       An About Us section that outlines your fight
        and why it's necessary.

-       Updates on your news and successes along the
        way, including any PR you receive.

-       All the social media content you create
        elsewhere.

-       A media section where journalists can find
        press releases and contact details.

-       Opinion pieces and guest posts from allies.

-       Tools for others to take action themselves.

DON'T
·DOWN
FEAR O
OFFENS
THE WOR
TAKE-IT-O
REVO
·

WATERED
THE
CAUSING
GIVE
D A
LEAVE - IT
UTION.

Be more human

Bill Gates has said that the internet is the town
square for our global village. And the ability of
all these social networks to bring people together
to share stories and suggest actions is a fantastic
advantage that today's revolutions enjoy.

But all these digital interactions can make us less
human. We can take on a different persona within
social media, as if these connections somehow abide
by different rules. So treat every moment as if your
audience is in the town square with you.

A place where we're considerate. We don't just make
demand after demand of people without giving anything
in return.

A place where we're conversational. We talk about
what's going on in the world. We bring up interesting
anecdotes. We don't just talk about ourselves.

A place where we're consistent. We know who we
are, what we believe in and the way we should talk
to people.

And remember that whatever corner of the internet you
find yourself in, it's just another town square.

Find your propaganda

By putting together
   your calendar
   (6A)
By getting social
   (6B)
By putting out lists
   (6C)
By creating awards
   (6D)
By creating digital
   placards
   (6E)

Find your propaganda by putting together your calendar

What is it?

Noise for your revolution can be created simply by using what's going on in the world.

How do I use it?

1. Start with a 12 month wall chart that has the whole year on one page.

2. Then head to daysoftheyear.com. Look for established events that you think might be interesting to create publicity around.

3. Scribble down any event you think could be useful on the calendar - you should be looking for about one a week.

4. Then start planning your publicity ahead. For each event, brainstorm how you could connect it to your revolution. Not everything you do has to be a big investment. Something as simple as a witty tweet, or a timely photo on Instagram might do the trick.

5. Finally, make sure your activity isn't all based around big events. There will be lots of noise at Christmas, the World Cup and Back to School. Make sure you have plenty of more obscure dates within your plan.

DAYS

OF THE

YEAR

.COM

Find_your_propaganda_by_getting_social

What is it?

Your online channels will act as a free media space
to show off all this propaganda. But each platform is
unique and requires a different formula.

How do I use it?

Rather than copying and pasting the same content into
every social channel, you need to think about how
you can make it native to each environment. This
means mimicking the aesthetic, tone and nature of the
content that people come to the platform to consume.

Instagram and Pinterest:
Where you have 1
second to be visually
aspirational

( ) Does my picture let
people say something
about themselves?
( ) Have I created an
image that is
as striking as it
can be?
( ) Does my picture fit
in with an existing
image trend?
( ) Is the image tagged
with clever comments
and witty hashtags?

Twitter:
Where you have 2 seconds
to be part of a trend

( ) Is it to the point?
( ) Is the hashtag unique
and as memorable as
it could be?
( ) Is there an image
that could be added?
( ) Is this new news for
the Twitter audience?

Facebook:
Where you have 3 seconds
to update the community

( ) Is the text pithy
enough?
( ) Is it provocative,
entertaining or
surprising?
( ) Is it in the right
format to post?
( ) Does it ask too much
of someone consuming
the content?

Medium and BuzzFeed:
Where you have 60 seconds
to make an argument

( ) Is it a beautifully
written case for
change?
( ) Does it make good
use of lists?
( ) Does this present a
jaw-dropping moment?
( ) Is there a way
for people to find
out more?

YouTube:
Where you have 10 seconds
to hook them with your
story

( ) Is it arresting from
the start?
( ) Are the production
values as good as
possible?
( ) Does it take the
viewer on a journey?
( ) Does it make people
feel a visceral
emotion?

Snapchat:
Where you have 24 hours
to show them behind the
scenes

( ) Is the content based
around a particular
moment in time?
( ) Does it have a
rough around the
edges authenticity?
( ) Does this provide
unique content
for those who've
followed me?
( ) Have I encouraged
others to find
the content from
elsewhere?

Find_your_propaganda_by_putting_out_lists

What is it?

Lists help distil why your revolution exists into
something really clear, which is easily picked up
and shared.

How do I use it?

Lists are about one thing - the ranking. Have a look
around BuzzFeed to get a sense of what gets people
excited and then think about what your own lists
could borrow from them.

It doesn't have to be heavy. Many top 10s are
irreverent and playful. Is there a way you can bring
a lightness of touch to things?

And keep it punchy. The beauty of lists is that they
are snackable content you can read, like and share
in under a minute.

1. _____   1. _____

2. _____   2. _____

3. _____   3. _____

4. _____   4. _____

5. _____   5. _____

1. _____   1. _____

2. _____   2. _____

3. _____   3. _____

4. _____   4. _____

5. _____   5. _____

1. _____   1. _____

2. _____   2. _____

3. _____   3. _____

4. _____   4. _____

5. _____   5. _____

Find_your_propaganda_by_creating_awards

What is it?

Creating awards is a quick and easy PR tactic to
pique the interest of readers and writers alike.

How do I use it?

First, you need a worthy winner. Don't go for who is
the most deserving; find who is the most newsworthy.
Remember that this might be because it's precisely
the sort of award you want to avoid (the Razzies now
get nearly as much publicity as the Oscars).

Another tactic that can generate interest is to let
others decide the winner. It's easy to set up a quick
poll and the voting process can generate publicity
in its own right.

Finally, your publicity depends on the recipient
getting proper recognition. So once you have your
winner, treat it as a real award. This could be as
simple as a certificate that you post as an image
online. But for a bigger splash, create a trophy or
even a fake awards ceremony.

Find your propaganda by creating digital placards

What is it?

Your revolution has a clear attitude that can be
liked, pinned and shared by others to tell the world
who they are.

How do I use it?

1.   Get inspired

There are plenty of images containing prophetic
wisdom already online. Have a look at Pinterest and
Instagram to see what's getting traction. Turn to
Brainyquote.com and Instagrammer thegoodquote to
see how the most inspiring communicators get their
beliefs across.

2.   Get writing

Go back to all the content you produced for the
rallying cry. Buried within that might be something
that wasn't snappy enough for that call to arms but
could be put to good use here. Pick out phrases.
Don't sit on the fence; the best ones won't just
sound great, they'll have an edge. Start putting them
in the squares below. Aim to use less than 40 words.

3.	Get art directing

Now give those words some life. Is there a striking
image that reinforces what you're saying? Should you
just consistently set your phrases in some beautiful
typography? Can you do both?

4.	Get sharing

Finally, get your creations up on our social
channels. But don't share them all at once; aim for
a regular rhythm of posts. And don't forget the
tagging - #quote #quotes #comment #comments #life
#quoteoftheday #funny #instagood #love #true

The first test -
Will someone share it?

Your propaganda relies on a viral effect. If it's
only ever seen by your closest followers, it won't
justify the time and effort that goes into creating
it. So challenge yourself. Would you like this or
pass it on? And keep an eye on your actual successes
- what gets measured gets done again.

The second test -
Is it mapped out?

There remains a limit on how much publicity you're
likely to generate. Overburden journalists and social
feeds and people will quickly tire of you, no matter
how worthy your intent. Build a 6-month plan. Colour
code your different types of propaganda - images,
surveys, press releases, awards, lists and so forth.
Is there a regular rhythm of news or is one colour or
month too densely packed?

The third test -
Is it native?

It can be tempting to copy and paste content across
each and every channel. But they all work in
different ways. You need to make sure your content
is appearing in the most appropriate place and not
simply every place. You may also find your revolution
gets more traction within one or two networks. If
this is the case, focus your efforts on being great
here rather than OK everywhere.

Notes

The Allies

You might be worried that letting anyone into your fight will dilute the vision. But for a revolution to succeed it needs to spread through a passionate community. It's these partners who will ultimately make change happen.

Not all allies will serve the same role. There will be an inner circle that join you from the start. 1000 true followers will kickstart your fame. And in time a network of networks will help you engage the masses.

Revolutions have always worked in this way, spreading through concentric circles of support. These communities will act as your media channel, your ideas factory and your insurance policy against criticism.

You need to know how to cultivate each group. And today this can happen in digital days rather than analogue years.

10 great places to find allies

Existing charity groups
and NGOs

Brands

Social structures, from
Girl Guides to football
clubs to Church groups

Media organisations,
from Vice to the Guardian
to BuzzFeed

Celebrities, whether
that's sporting heroes,
pop stars or comedians

Funding organisations
and philanthropists

Politicians and
government organisations

Others making change
in 'sister movements'

Universities and students

Academics, think tanks
and policy makers

Not all allies serve the same role

It's important to think about the role each group
of allies serves. Once you understand what they can
bring to your crusade, you'll be able to arm them
accordingly so that they can most effectively build
and spread the revolution.

Your inner circle will join you from the beginning,
forming the very backbone of the revolution itself.
The foundations they provide will cover everything
from credibility to complementary skills to guidance.

The two other sets of allies will help the revolution
to spread. 1000 true followers will be your most
ardent supporters - involved, engaged and deeply
connected. But to get such commitment you'll need to
motivate them to begin with.

Finally, there's your network of networks. Whilst
these allies will be less engaged, they carry
strength in numbers. Channelled in the right way they
can provide a vital role spreading the word, building
your brand and even raising funds.

LONE

WOLVES

TO STA

WITH T

PACK YO

END.
E. HUNT
HUNGRIEST
CAN FIND.

The inner circle: find some trusted comrades

Whereas other allies will help spread your
revolution, the inner circle will shape its very DNA.
These are your closest partners, brought in to offer
vital experience you're missing:

Gaps

It's unlikely you have all the skills to make the
revolution happen. Not every great visionary is a
great doer. Maybe you need a manager to complement
you. If you don't feel comfortable with the
accounting side of things, find someone who does.
If you're not going to be the public face of your
revolution, find the face that fits.

Often these skills relate to one of two areas. You
might have someone close to an issue who needs
partners that can help turn their fight into a brand.
The better the brand, the bigger the revolution. If
you can't do the creative work yourself, bringing in
partners who can tends to pay back.

Or it might be the other way round. You're a brand
that has identified your crusade but you need
to bring in an expert. Someone who knows the issue
inside out can shine the light on exactly what needs
to be done to change things.

Guards

An essential part of planning your revolution is to
think about how you might counter any criticism.
Partnering with credible allies is often the best
form of defence.

This is especially true for brands that are seeking commercial gains out of social causes. The answer tends to be working with charities in that field. These partners can also offer practical help. Pampers didn't provide vaccines for infants themselves but outsourced the solution on the ground to Unicef. The relationship provided them with both the credibility and the solution.

Guides

All creative enterprises need someone to bounce ideas off. A comrade who isn't wound up in the day-to-day of the revolution can provide a fresh pair of eyes and a valuable sense of perspective.

Pixar call this their Brain Trust. Every film in development is pitched to a group of experienced directors, animators and producers who've already enjoyed success. They offer feedback, but crucially those on the receiving end still enjoy complete autonomy. They can choose to hang off every word of advice, or reject it completely.

So think about how you can replicate this pressure-free culture and openness with your mentors. See if you can start with someone who has already done it. People are amazingly generous with their knowledge and experience if you ask them for it gracefully.

How to find a buffer: SAINSBURY'S

On the 100th anniversary of the First World War
Christmas Day truce, Sainsbury's recreated one of
the famous scenes for their campaign. Soldiers
from both sides ceased hostilities for a brief while
to play football. It showed the true spirit
of Christmas.

Sainsbury's also knew they might be in for some flak
from anyone who thought they were glorifying war
for commercial ends. So to insure themselves against
criticism, they partnered with the Royal British
Legion. Money from sales of the commemorative
chocolate bar featured in the advert went to the
charity. They couldn't be anything other than a
supporter of veterans.

The following year their Christmas advert promoted
reading for children. This time their partner was
Save the Children's literacy programme. £2 from every
£3 book sold went to the charity and it was that
Christmas's best seller.

1000 True Followers: three fans at a time

It's been found that an artist can make a living from just the 1000 fans that purchase everything they put out. And if you can get 1000 True Followers on board, their commitment is all that's needed to start spreading your revolution.

You're after the ones who will share your propaganda. The ones that will convince their friends to take out your action. The ones that will become your army of creators.

The way most people go about trying to drum up support is top down. They shoot for a certain amount of traffic, and hope to convert a proportion of these. But not everybody is going to connect with what you do at that insatiable level. You need to identify those that are most likely to take up arms.

Map everyone else who is likely to be receptive to your crusade. Start with those who've already got in touch. Then brainstorm the key voices on your issue. Charities, influencers, journalists. Think tanks, celebrities and brands. Learn who is who, and consider how their own plans could align with yours.

One thousand might seem like a stretch, but it's far from impossible. It's one person in every town in Britain. It's three people a day for a year. It's 0.005% of David Beckham's Instagram followers.

Rallying True Followers isn't easy, but it is simple
- you just need to make people feel like they belong.

Give them motivation

Robert Burns said that the purpose of life is a life
of purpose. You can instill this drive in others
when you make them feel as though they're the only
ones that understand the fight.

Give them mystery

Part of belonging is knowing that others don't.
It's why the LA Bloods gang wear red, whilst their
rivals the Crips wear blue. Create a similar
sense of enigma around your revolution. Use codes,
symbols and secrets.

Give them momentum

Fans roar loudest when they see that their songs
are having an impact on the team. So let your army
of support know that they're making a difference.

1000 True Followers: moving from creator to conductor

Many people are drawn towards revolutions by the thought that their own creativity could make a difference. When supporters turn into creators it binds them even tighter.

There are lots of outlets for this self-expression. YouTube is there for budding film makers. Instagram appeals to the photographers and illustrators. Medium rewards the speechwriter. Your revolution can offer their output a much wider audience.

So raise the call to arms. Ask your followers to get creative. Tell them what you need. Reward them with fame. And pull everything together with common hashtags and a central online home.

Your revolution is well placed to benefit from this shift to open-source communications. The action, symbol and rallying cry can act as your own source code. A consistent DNA, so that everything created stays true to your brand.

There's a lot of noise out there; your role is to conduct the orchestra towards music that rises above it. Just don't lose sense of the melody. A few bum notes will soon ruin your harmonies.

How to give your supporters autonomy: OBAMA

The campaign to elect President Obama turned the
conventional campaigning programme on its head. It
did away with command and control from its leader
and embraced the inspiration that was bubbling up at
a grassroots level.

Ordinary people were encouraged to set up their
own local chapters and become self-appointed local
campaign managers. It empowered volunteers to talk
to potential supporters directly. It entrusted them
with fundraising.

But none of this diluted the coherence of Obama's
vision. The iconography was clearly defined. The
themes of HOPE and CHANGE were central to everything.
The policies were watertight. And all this meant
supporters could enjoy more freedom in how they got
them across.

By dispersing responsibilities this widely, the
Obama movement expanded its reach much further than
it could have done with the traditional top-down
approach. But more importantly, it gave everyday
people a real stake in the campaign. Which generated
a level of passion that no other political campaign
had ever seen.

A Network of Networks: your Big Black Book

The final allies are any existing networks that
can swell your supporter base. Whether they are
involved in your issue or not, the important thing
is that they can help spread the fight faster than
you could alone.

You need to make it as easy as possible for any
allies to be involved. So when you hand them an ask,
hand them a tool as well.

Don't just ask students to show their support -
provide the posters for them to print off and display
in their dorms.

Don't just ask church groups to write to their
MP - provide the letter template that they can
each customise.

Don't just ask mums to lobby advertisers - provide
the script for them to use when they call.

Challenge yourself. What's the smallest ask you
could make of any ally that provides the biggest
possible bang in terms of the publicity it generates?

And take time to craft a compelling pitch. Show
humility and politeness. Tailor your message by
showing why you think they could help. Provide
a clear and easy ask of them. But do ask. Even if
you have to kiss a lot of frogs.

How to find a sympathetic audience: NO MORE PAGE 3

If No More Page 3 was all about equal representation
for women, the Girl Guides had over 500,000 young
ones finding their way in the world.

One of the Guides' core objectives is to give girls
a voice on the issues that matter to them. And their
advocates group decided the organisation should lend
their support.

Members signed the petition in their thousands. They
posted pictures of support to their Facebook accounts.
They blogged, tweeted and commented on why they were
supporting the campaign.

One Guide cared so much that she even managed to get
an interview on Radio 4's Today programme.

Similar successes have been enjoyed by Movember with
sports clubs and the Moonwalk against Breast Cancer
with women's guilds. Neither was directly involved in
the issues to begin with, but the important thing was
that they shared an audience.

<u>How to target influencers: BRING BACK OUR GIRLS</u>

Over 2000 young girls had already been abducted by
Boko Haram. But when 276 girls were taken from the
village of Chibok in Northern Nigeria, the hashtag
#bringbackourgirls ensured that this time the
world took notice.

Its success was thanks to the campaigning of Oby
Ezekwesili. Her anger at the lack of action in her
own country drove her to start using the hashtag.
Writing to prominent female campaigners she
hoped would be sympathetic to her cause, she asked
them to show support by using the hashtag.

One of those was Sarah Brown, wife of the former
Prime Minister. When she shared her own
#bringbackourgirls message, it triggered a domino
effect. Before long, it was trending around
the world.

In less than three weeks the hashtag had been used
over 1 million times. Everyone from supermodel Cara
Delevingne to Michelle Obama added their selfies to
the mounting social media anger.

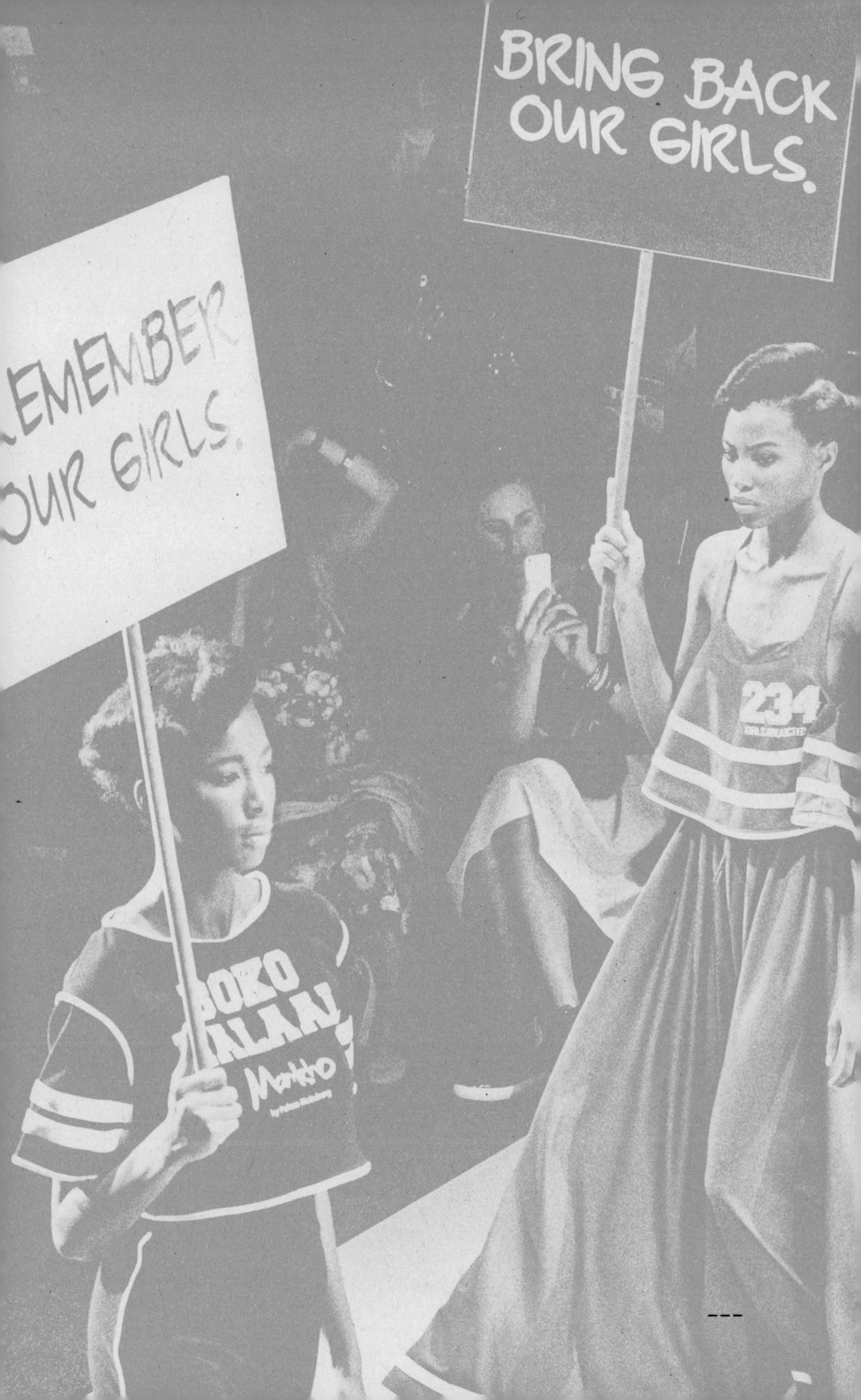
BRING BACK
OUR GIRLS.
EMEMBER
OUR GIRLS.
234

A Network of Networks: surprise is the oldest tactic

You may find the most newsworthy associations lie
outside your immediate sphere. If your revolution
is about getting kids active, those directly
linked to the fight might not pique the interest of
a journalist.

So try moving onto groups that share a similar
audience. Perhaps you look at child literacy and
consider what you could gain from alliances with
them. Could physical exercise help you learn to read
at the same time? That starts to sound interesting.

Or what about brands that target kids? Don't think
about who they are, think about what you could
do. Maybe you start to develop a new range of Barbies
that encourage an active lifestyle.

Finally, challenge yourself with the most unlikely
association you could make. Force yourself to think
as laterally as possible. You probably think your
enemy is the very last person you'd want onboard but
maybe they're the ones that could really help.

A TV channel tends to keep its audience sedentary.
But when ITV turned off all programming on the first
Saturday after the Olympics, one million people
left their living rooms to take part in sport. I am
Team GB was the country's biggest ever sports day.

As ever, it's the ideas and not the fight that will
get partners excited. Don't just draw up a list of
potential alliances: develop a pitch that shows them
the potential of a win-win.

How to forge surprising alliances: GREENLIGHT A VET

Walmart was committed to helping war veterans
transition back into civilian life. It had already
committed to hire 250,000 vets but wanted to turn
its own shoppers into allies too.

They knew that most of their shoppers valued the
contribution of veterans, both during and following
service. But actually showing this appreciation was
another matter.

The answer was to ask of them just one simple change.
The change of a lightbulb.

Switching to a green lightbulb provided a visible
symbol of their support. The green represented
forward momentum. A call that their life was moving
forward once they left the military.

And because Walmart had over 6,000 stores that could
sell them, it made doing so easy. They didn't just
make an ask; they provided the solution.

```
--------------------------
Find your allies

By developing 1000 True
    Followers
    (7A)
By asking other networks
    to help
    (7B)
```

<u>Find_your_allies_by_developing_1000_True_Followers</u>

What is it?

When you can inspire 1000 True Followers to get on
board, their commitment can be all that's needed to
kickstart your revolution.

How do I use it?

The chances of getting 1000 followers with a shotgun
approach are pretty slim. You need to start mapping
who will be receptive to your crusade. Start by
trying to get 100 actual names.

Take the time to brainstorm the key voices on the
issue. Learn who is who, and consider how their plans
could align with yours. Get to 10 names in each
category. Then ask each of these for 10 further names
and you're well on your way to 1000.

THE REV-OLU-TION

Existing change advocates relating to the issue	Brands with clear proximities	Influencers with an interest	Non-profit partners and NGO's	Media with similar viewpoints
eg. Stop Whaling Now!	Marks and Spencer	Prince Charles	Greenpeace	The Guardian
1.				
2.				
3.				
4.				
5.				
6.				
7.				
8.				
9.				
10.				

Celebrity advocates	Government	Think tanks and lobbyists	Scientists and academics	Creators
Heston Blumenthal	Elizabeth Truss MP	Human Dimensions Think Tank	Southampton Uni Marine Biology Dpt	Britdoc

---

Find your allies by asking other networks to help

What is it?

Gaining access to existing networks can quickly
multiply your own supporter base. But you
need to tailor your request to the individual or
organisation concerned.

IMPARTIAL

PEOPLE

SPECIFIC ASKS
FOR INFLUENTIAL
INDIVIDUALS

MUTUAL
BENEFITS
FOR
COMMITTED
GROUPS

SMALL ASKS
FOR ENGAGED
INDIVIDUALS

EXCITING
REQUESTS
FOR SYNERGISTIC
GROUPS

ORGANI-
SATIONS

INVOLVED

How do I use it?

Brainstorm who you could contact within each of the four categories. You're trying to reach a sizeable network of other people. Once you have a list of names, start working out what you're asking of each:

Small asks for engaged individuals

These might be academics, politicians or high-profile campaigners that are involved in your issue already and likely to be short on time. The smaller your ask, the more likely you are to get a yes.

Specific asks for influential individuals

These might be celebrities, social media stars or figures of influence. They might not be linked to your cause, but they will command large followings you wish to access. Give them the specific request that will best serve your publicity.

Mutual benefits for committed groups

These might be charities and NGOs, trade unions, academic institutions or businesses. Call out how they can help and see if there's a mutual benefit you can create for each other.

Exciting requests for synergistic groups

These might be media owners, faith groups or social organisations like sports clubs. Rather than already being involved in your fight the wins here come from other synergies. So think about how you could use their audience in a way that's most exciting for them.

The first test -
Do you have all you need?

We tend to turn to others in times of need. So do
some disaster planning. If you were under attack,
would you have the right credibility? If you really
needed advice, is there an old hand you can call on?
When you desperately need publicity, have you got
all the creative partners you require? Challenging
yourself on these questions will ensure the right
inner circle is in place.

The second test -
Is it easy for people to join?

No matter how deeply people might care, human
nature means that actually taking action is always
more challenging. What easy actually means will
vary depending on who you're asking. It might mean
ensuring a celebrity has a T-shirt in three different
sizes so that they're more likely wear one that fits.
Or it might mean that signing up to your news is no
more complicated than entering an email address. Go
through all of your potential allies and think about
how you can lubricate their involvement.

The third test -
Have you let go?

Ultimately it will be the power of the people
that creates the change you seek. Revolutions are
democratic. They are open. They create movement from
the bottom up. But this can only happen when you
are confident enough to hand the building blocks of
the revolution over to them. When you do, you'll
find that many hands (and voices) make light work.

Notes

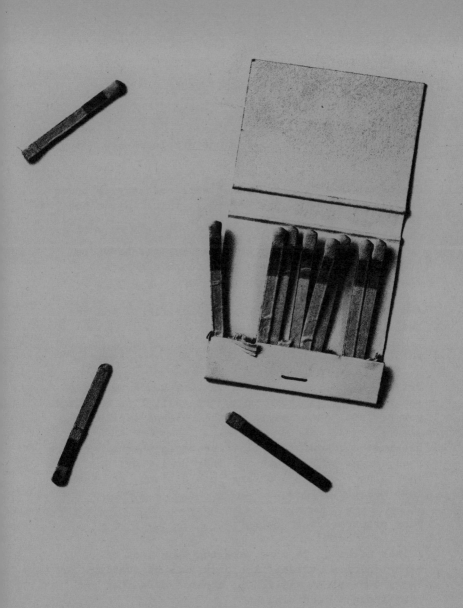

Fear shouldn't be your biggest enemy

99% of revolutions fail for one simple reason - they never start.

Coming up with the ideas that will create your brand is relatively easy. The difficult thing is making them happen.

The right moment rarely arrives. But the barriers come round all too often. Not enough money, not enough experience, not enough time.

And once you do go public with your fight, you can be judged. And you can fail.

But, here's a trick.

Write a newspaper headline. The one you'd see when you win the fight. Pin it to the wall. It's amazing how powerful just imagining that change can be.

The most successful revolutions begin whether they're ready or not. They have to. They're lit by the one thing that turns dreams into actions, and ideas into reality.

They are sparked by belief.

A lack of faith is more damaging than lack of experience, a lack of time or a lack of funding. But carry conviction and you'll achieve more than you ever thought possible.

If fear is progress's sterilizer, then belief can be its fertilizer. Find your spark. Get going today. You'll find it's the magical eighth ingredient.

It's_great_when_you're_a_revolting_person

You have	You don't have
Dynamism	Red tape
Authenticity	Politics
Courage	Expectations

Australian nurse Bronnie Ware recorded the epiphanies
of her patients. She found that the biggest regret
people had looking back on their lives was that they
hadn't fulfilled their dreams.

Most of us enjoy a freedom that's easy to take for
granted until it's taken away. Starting a revolution
helps you look back safe in the knowledge that you
made a difference.

What's more, when a person performs an act of kindness the brain produces endorphins. Think of these as
natural versions of heroin. They make you feel good
on a chemical level.

Working with others also forms an emotional bond,
which produces oxytocin and causes the dilation of
the arteries.

So it's not just about legacy; science tells us that
revolting can lead to higher levels of health and
happiness day to day.

It's great when you're a revolting charity

You have	You don't have
Followers	Cynicism
Credibility	A commercial agenda
A mission	Resistance

Whilst consumers can be pleasantly surprised to see a brand doing good, they expect that behaviour from a charity. But this means they can also be taken for granted. A revolution acts as the rocket launcher that shoots a charity into the imagination of millions.

This can provide a spike in giving. Revolutions are becoming central to the fundraising of charities like Oxfam and the ALS Association, who might otherwise suffer from 'giving blindness'.

This can provide an opportunity to get across your message. Rather than being always on, revolutions provide a window where people sit up and listen. Movements like Fair Trade Fortnight are time bound for this reason.

Most importantly, this can provide the actions you need for change. Revolutions direct huge audiences towards doing something. They create an urgency. They make things happen.

It's great when you're a revolting brand

You have	You don't have
Money	Bureaucracy
Experience	Pressure
Ambition	Orthodoxies

Great brands have always added to our lives. Tide
created the first soap operas. Guinness wrote
the Book of Records. Mr Kipling invented a mythical
baker. But today that dent in culture is more
likely to come from a dog adoption scheme or a
vaccination programme.

For some time, society has been trending towards
greater empathy and citizen engagement. Brands won't
benefit from this shift through corporate social
responsibility or a spot of charitable giving. Doing
the right thing has become a hygiene factor. It no
longer gets you attention.

Today it's the pro-social brands turning around
relevant social and environmental issues that are
turning heads. Instead of focusing on what they've
done internally, they're looking at what they could
do in the wider world.

And their weapon of choice isn't a commercial
or a campaign. It's a revolution. A new way of
communicating that invites its audience to impact the
world they live in. Communications that are creating
more fame and feeling for the brand with fewer costs
to the business.

IF YOU A
FIND A
ROUTE, Y
FIND SI
TO ANY
WORTH

ET LOST,
NEW'
U WON'T
'RT CUTS
HERE
GOING.

<u>Don't fail before you've begun</u>

It's possible that you've put together the seven
components but your revolution is still stalling.
It fails to build the scale or momentum that's needed
to really rally the masses. And it never creates
real change.

If this is the case, there are three common traps
that you may have fallen into.

Are you being too literal?

Don't make the mistake of thinking doing good is
enough to capture people's attention. You need something that will capture their hearts. Bring something
new and unexpected to the crusade.

Are you being too vague?

The easiest way to lose people is to ensure they
don't know what you stand for or what you're trying
to achieve.

Are you being too fake?

Stay true to who you are. Make sure you have your own
house in order. And don't take credit where it isn't
due. If people think you're just spinning your
own agenda, they'll be far less forgiving of mistakes.

How to avoid being too literal: THE GLOBAL MOMS
CHALLENGE VS THIS GIRL CAN

Johnson and Johnson were fighting alongside the UN
for a world where all women and their children could
lead healthy lives.

As their action, the Global Moms Relay asked them
to share stories of the kind of future they wanted
to see.

The problem was that these stories were just so
predictable. They were each highly aspirational and
told with real passion, but it felt like a lecture.
They didn't add any interest or magic.

Without a new twist, the films failed the 'make it
interesting' challenge. Viewing was limited to the
hundreds rather than hitting the millions. So the
relay failed to change any behaviours.

Contrast this with This Girl Can from Sport England.
Another revolution fighting for women's health, by
encouraging them back into exercise. And again, real
stories from real women.

But this time the women were turned into rock stars.
The dynamic film they were featured in was bold,
empowering and full of attitude. It felt fresh. It
made you want to get up and join in. Which is exactly
what women did.

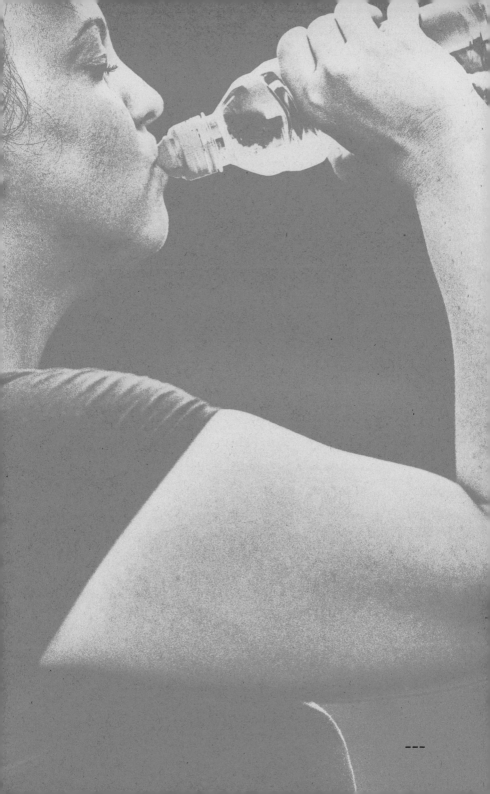

When the Labour leader Ed Miliband unveiled a 12ft granite election oath he hoped that the country would take it as a sign of his commitment. The problem was that they were built around the woolly vision of 'a better plan, a better future'. The six pledges that sat under it were just as vague.

That same week, the Conservatives revealed a very simple poster showing a tiny Miliband poking out of the pocket of the Scottish National Party leader. Their message was strikingly clear: voting in a Labour Prime Minister would provide a puppet for the SNP.

Rather than playing with ambiguous clichés, it went straight for the main fear of many English voters. For many this marked the turning point that ultimately led to the Tories winning power.

UK ELECTION DEBATE
Seven party leaders taking pa

BBC WORLD NEWS ROMISES'

How to avoid being too fake: MCDONALD'S VS BREWDOG

McDonald's had received praise from many American gay rights groups for their support of Pride events in the USA.

But when they didn't join other brands in condemning Russia's anti-gay laws during the Sochi Winter Olympics they faced criticism. Especially when people realised they were an Olympic sponsor.

The criticism soon turned to activism. The website cheerstosochi.org was set up with a near identical web address to McDonald's own cheerstosochi.com. It became the place for people to confront the brand about their lack of concern for LGBT rights in Russia.

Visitors to the site were encouraged to create memes. Many combined images of the sponsor's brand mascots with pictures of gay people who had been beaten up in homophobic attacks. All were shared using McDonald's #CheerstoSochi hashtag.

Compare this to the campaign from the brewer Brewdog. Russia had banned 'homosexual propaganda', so they simply did the opposite. Hello My Name is Vladimir was an IPA containing limonnik berries, an ingredient thought by some Russian hunters to enhance men's sexual performance. It was marketed as #NotForGays. And it just happened to carry an image of the Russian premier wearing make-up on the label.

Their tongue-in-cheek approached worked. The craft brewery was well known for its provocative and risky marketing. So if they had taken a different approach it would have seemed insincere. Instead drinkers, journalists and LGBT groups loved the way the beer

mocked the laws whilst simultaneously bypassing them.
The ingredients label noted that the product may
contain traces of sarcasm. They even sent a case to
Mr Putin himself. And 50% of profits went directly to
charities representing oppressed LGBT groups around
the world. A different drink, a different campaign
and an altogether different response.

As a brand, if you're not straight with people you'll
be found out and possibly punished. Nobody expects
marketers to start revolutions out of pure altruism.
But you need to make sure your other actions don't
contradict what you're seeking to achieve. And, as we
said before, never take credit where it isn't due.

You may find sustaining a revolution to be harder
than starting one. The trickiest phase tends to
be around the halfway point. Some of the novelty
has worn off, but there's still a long way to go.
Problems can crop up. Or worse still, doubt can set
in. So before you start, learn how to finish.

Look to others

When you find yourself freewheeling you'll eventually
run out of momentum. So use the ideas and energy of
your followers to keep the revolution moving forward.
Get as many brains back on the problem as you can.

Look within

There are many lies you can tell your revolution.
I don't have enough time, I don't have enough
experience, I don't have enough money, I don't have
enough guts. Relocate the conviction that made
you start this to begin with. It will still be in
there somewhere.

Look on the bright side

When you drive a race car, if you look at the wall
you will probably drive straight into it. If you
focus on how your revolution might fail, there's
every chance you will. If you look at how far you've
come, you'll stay on track.

Look behind

For years, the appeals run by children's TV show Blue
Peter have used the totaliser to show week-by-week
progress. If people can see that you're also moving

forward it will act as a motivational shot in the
arm. Capture your successes, but show that there is
still work to be done.

Look after yourself

The first piece of advice Patti Smith gives young
artists is go to the dentist. So get some sleep.
Exercise. Eat well. Laugh. You need to work hard, but
you need to work the right way.

Look ahead

You won't change anything. The four most poisonous
words any revolutionary can hear. And it's exactly
the same words the British Raj told Gandhi. There
will always be naysayers. But it can be done, it has
been done and chances are you're doing it too. Even
if you don't know it yet.

LEARN
YOUR HA
THEY
YOU'RE S
UP FOR

O LOVE
ERS;
MEAN
ANDING
SOMETHING.

Critics are a byproduct of success

Sometimes the naysayers can go beyond mere doubt.
If your revolution tackles an issue where others
have strong interests it can lead to abuse and
sniping. Perhaps even threats from a small-minded
few desperate for some publicity of their own.

Ignoring it is the easiest option. The negative
stuff is likely to account for a tiny proportion of
the feedback you're receiving. Not doing anything
keeps your focus on the fight.

Even if you take this stand, it is often worth
reporting it. This can block the perpetrator on
social media, removing their primary weapon.
And if things do escalate, you can consider the
police. The law states that 'communications which
are grossly offensive, indecent, false or carry
credible threats' are criminal.

Finally, consider whether your fight can be
strengthened through leveraging it. With a bit
of imagination, social media allows you to turn
that abuse into publicity. It will highlight the
absurdity of those who are fighting against you.

<u>Turn 20 into 80</u>

It's rare that anyone feels they have enough time
for their revolution. But we can also spend most
of our time on the things that make the least
difference. Typically 80% of our time falls into
this camp. So you don't need more time; you need to
grow that other 20% doing what you're brilliant at.

Start by writing down where you think your time has
the biggest impact. Speaking to influencers, writing
press releases, Instagramming... whatever you think
is most effective at spreading the fame and impact
of the revolution.

Now start another column of all the things that
take up too much time and provide too little reward.
Surfing the web, making unfocused requests, holding
meetings without clear outputs, replying to emails,
accounts. Again, be as exhaustive as possible.

The challenge is then to work out how you can spend
more time on what's working and less time on what's
not. When you have a tactic that is creating real
impact, set yourself ambitious goals around them.
If your mindbombs work, then turn one a year into
one a month. If speaking to influencers works, then
challenge yourself to speak to one more each week.

The same goes for the drains. Put a line through
things you just need to cut out. You won't be able
to remove everything, so work out if there's a
way someone else could help. It might mean ceding
some control, but if it allows you to focus on the
things that are delivering the most impact it will
be worth it.

DON'T
BE TRUE
DON'T
THE FASH
INVE
DON'T
STAN

COOL,

FOLLOW

N,

JT IT.

TAND STILL

OUT.

You don't have much time

You have roughly 28,835 days on this planet. Maybe a few more, maybe a few less. But this is the average.

By the time we reach adulthood, there are 23,360 left.

We'll sleep for 8,477 of these.

We'll eat for 1,635.

We'll be at work for 3,302.

1,099 will be spent commuting or travelling.

We'll spend 2,676 watching TV (and that's a lot of Netflix).

Household chores will take 1,576.

Looking after the needs of others takes another 564.

We'll even spend 671 days in the bathroom.

Take all these away, and we have 2,740 days.

Each of those days gives you 1,440 minutes in credit. Everyone has the same, but we are each free to spend them as we see fit.

But the thing about this currency is we can't make any more. It's limited. There are no refunds. No investments. No sale and return.

So, you have to ask. Did I use my time well? Did I do what mattered to me? Did I make the change I'd hoped?

<u>You have lots of time</u>

On May 25th 1961 President Kennedy stood before
Congress and declared that the USA would put a man on
the moon before the end of the decade.

We choose to go to the moon, he told the world. And
most of the world thought he was mad.

It was only three years earlier that anyone had
managed to get a satellite into space. Now he was
promising that not only would man head up there,
but he'd set foot on solid rock. In eight years time.

The first human flight was still a recent memory
for many. A flying machine built by a pair of
brothers and some bike parts. It had flown 37 metres.

Now the plan was to travel 250,000 miles. It seemed
like lunacy.

And yet, just 2,502 days later there was one small
step for man.

We tend to overestimate how much we can achieve in
a short space of time and underestimate what we can
achieve over longer periods.

So aim for the moon. You may miss and hit a star.

All revolutions begin as storms brewing in the minds
of people who want change. They start with a no and
end with a yes.

If you tremble with indignation at an injustice,
you'll find others will too. And the brand you create
will turn that spark into an explosion of change.

But fear sterilises progress. Anyone can what-if
themselves into inertia. Maybe you've got to the end
of this book and you still have doubts. After all,
the impostor syndrome runs deep in most of us.

So grab a piece of paper and write your Worst Case
Scenario list. Get them down, all your largest fears.

Then walk yourself through each one and assign a how
bad value and a how likely value. Give each a score
out of 10. Think hard. Would they really criticise
you? And if they did, how do you feel about that?
Could you not undo that decision?

You'll now have a list of the things standing in your
way. But you'll also know just how bad these are, and
how likely they are to happen.

Now flip the paper over and do the same on the other
side. But this time for your Best Case Scenario.
What would happen if you achieved your goal? What
would be the impact on your issue, your career, your
happiness? And what would happen if you were just
50% successful?

If that first side of paper is more scary than the
second one is inspiring, then maybe the revolution
isn't for you.

But if that's not the case, what are you waiting for? Failing isn't the worst thing that can happen. The worst thing would be if you didn't even try.

The truth is that all revolutions start out phony before they become real. And it's only once you're a fully fledged revolutionary that you'll realise you're no longer pretending to make a difference, but you actually are.

Another thing Tolstoy wrote in his letter to Gandhi was that 'history should more accurately be considered an infinitely large number of infinitesimally small actions'.

Make sure yours is one of them. Brand the change you want to see in the world.

IT'S TI
TAKE O
MAKE SUR
NOT S
COMP

ME TO

. PLEASE

YOU'RE

TTING

ORTABLY.

---

5 4 3

Activism

- 38degrees.org.uk
- Change.org
- Doing Good Better,
  Dr William MacAskill

Blogging

- Medium.com
- Wordpress.com
- Tumblr.com

Branding

- Changing the world
  is the only fit
  work for a grown man,
  Steve Harrison
- Business for Punks,
  James Watt
- The responsible
  company,
  Yvon Chouinard

Community

- Nationbuilder.com
- Facebook.com
- Mailchimp.com

Design

- Behance.com
- 99designs.com

Fundraising

- Crowdrise.com
- Kickstarter.com
- Shopify.com

Presentations

- Prezi.com
- Talk Like TED,
  Carmine Gallo

Idea generation

- Buzzsumo.com
- Portent.com/tools/
  title-maker
- Hubspot.com/blog-
  topic-generator
- How to have
  great ideas,
  John Ingledew
- Show your work,
  Austin Kleon

Inspiration

- Buzzfeed.com/world
- Nextdraft.com
- Thedolectures.com/talks
- Ted.com
- Collectively.org
- This.cm
- Medium.com/matter
- Good.is

Photography

- Flickr.com/
  creativecommons
- Imcreator.com/free
- Gimp.org

Presentations

- Prezi.com
- Talk Like TED,
  Carmine Gallo

Productivity

- Slack.com
- The 4-Hour Workweek,
  Tim Ferriss
- Sprint,
  Jake Knapp
- Calm,
  Michael Acton Smith

Research

- Surveymonkey.com
- Quora.com
- Askwonder.com

Revolutionaries

- Start something that
  matters,
  Blake Mycoskie
- The Promise of
  a Pencil,
  Adam Braun
- The story of my
  experiments with
  the truth,
  M.K. Gandhi
- Warriors of the
  Rainbow,
  Robert Hunter
- Winter on Fire, 2015

Scrapbooks

- Getpocket.com
- Pinterest.com
- Evernote.com

Statistics

- Yougov.co.uk/results
- Ons.gov.uk
- Public.tableau.com
- Piktochart.com
- Google.co.uk/trends
- Silk.co

Writing

- Grammarly.com
- Hemingwayapp.com
- Save the Cat,
  Blake Snyder
- Can I change
  your mind?,
  Lindsay Camp

Tomasz Bidermann/ Shutterstock.com	011
nito/ Shutterstock.com	013
Iryna Papina/ Shutterstock.com	015
Elena Mirage/ Shutterstock.com Vlad Karavaev/ Shutterstock.com	017
Anchiy/ Shutterstock.com	018
Eugenio Marongiu/ Shutterstock.com	023
Hadrian/ Shutterstock.com	027
Suzanne Tucker/ Shutterstock.com	041
Alliance/ Shutterstock.com	057
Roshnee Desai	059
Vicki Couchman	103
Remus Moise/ Shutterstock.com	110

About the Authors

Alex Lewis

Alex has created advertising strategies for some of
the most iconic global brands. He earned his stripes
at Ogilvy and BBDO, developing some of the most
awarded advertising of the past decade for brands
like Snickers and Guinness. The company he founded
has been called 'the Agency of Record for the people
changing the world'.

Bridget Angear

Bridget has been recognised as one of the world's
leading advertising strategists. She has worked for
JWT and BBDO, leading government campaigns like
Think! and organ donation, alongside brands like
Pepsi and Walkers. She helped create Make Poverty
History, which secured an extra $50billion in G8
pledges fighting global poverty.